DAILY MEDITATIONS

for Practicing

THE COURSE

Karen Casey

A HAZELDEN BOOK

HarperSanFrancisco
An Imprint of HarperCollins*Publishers*

OTHER TITLES BY THIS AUTHOR

Each Day a New Beginning
The Promise of a New Day
A Woman's Spirit

The ideas represented in this text are the author's interpretation and
not necessarily endorsed by the Foundation for Inner Peace, the
publisher and copyright holder of *A Course in Miracles*.®

FIRST HARPERCOLLINS EDITION PUBLISHED IN 1995

Library of Congress Cataloging-in-Publication Data

Casey, Karen.
Daily meditations for practicing the Course / Karen Casey
"A Hazelden book."
ISBN: 0–06–255276–7 (pbk.)
1. Course in miracles—Meditations. 2. Spiritual life—Meditations.
3. Devotional calendars. I. Title.
BP605.C68C37 1995   95-12829
299'.93—dc20

96 97 98 99 00 ❖ HAD 10 9 8 7 6 5 4 3

Giving and receiving are one in the same,
whether sheltering shame, projecting blame
. . . or extending peace by any name.
So in place of each face of humankind,
Let's see a healing heart and mending mind . . .
that the blessing we believe and give
may be ours to receive and Live.
Thanks.

—G.M.

ACKNOWLEDGMENTS

I owe many people a debt of gratitude for their support of me, not only with this book but with my entire, evolving personhood. My husband, Joe, comes first to mind. What a holy journey we're on! It's full of love, laughter, and learning. It has also had its share of struggle, growth, and pain. We're wonderfully matched learning partners. We're so lucky.

My friends in Twelve Step programs have always supported me emotionally and spiritually. They are present in my heart every time I write.

I am grateful to the Foundation for Inner Peace for having published *A Course in Miracles.*® It has absolutely changed my life.

And thanks to George, my mentor, whose vision and clarity regarding the *Course,* and thus "this dream," lend a radiance to every minute spent in his presence. My many friends in study groups have offered me immeasurable enlightenment along with much needed comic relief. Besty, Rinnie, Joe, Helen, Kathy, Mary, Virginia, Robert, Alberta, Beverly, Becky, and Mike, to name just a few, are very much present in this book and my life. Together we are journeying home and we need each other to find our way. For all of them and all of you, I'm grateful. Let's continue the trip.

INTRODUCTION

I've written numerous books over the last fifteen years, books that relate to my personal growth and spiritual development as a woman recovering from addiction, but none of them have been closer to my heart than the one you are now holding. Actually, that's not surprising. I firmly believe that one's life evolves like an educational program. When we become ready for the next series of lessons, they beckon and we eagerly or reluctantly move toward them. That's how it came to pass that *A Course in Miracles*® got my attention.

I want to be honest with you. I didn't savor the *Course* initially. In fact, my first reading of the workbook, in 1981, triggered both intellectual and emotional resistance. I found more passages that I could take exception to than embrace. However, I also sensed something was there for me. I am so grateful that the ego didn't put up too much of a fight. Or perhaps my inner "decision maker" was more committed to a spiritual path than placating the ego. For whatever reason, I eventually returned to this journey, and my life and all my relationships have been abundantly rewarded.

If you are a serious student of the *Course,* are anticipating joining a study group, or are pursuing the books on your own, you are in for an exhilarating experience, one that will deepen and enrich your life daily. Learning that *miracles* are little more than simple shifts in how we perceive our lives, other people, and the myriad situations that engage us makes it possible to thoroughly appreciate every moment of a day. For most of us, that's a phenomenal change. Seldom have we been able to glean "the miraculous" from even the most pleasurable experiences. And now, at will, we can claim that as our right in every experience.

It's important that I not mislead you, however. Studying *A Course in Miracles*® isn't easy. Often the message, whether in the text or the workbook, is directly opposite to what the ego tells us. And we are far more used to listening to the ego than accepting the wisdom of the Holy Spirit. What has worked best for me is not to pressure myself. If I can't understand what I'm reading or hearing at a study group, I let it go for a while. The concept will rise again. In fact, each principle gets repeated many, many times, just as many times as is necessary for us to understand them. Patience and perseverance will pay off. We're told in the text that we have all the time we need; there is no hurry. Deciding to believe this statement offered me a lot of relief. Also, reading sections from the manual for teachers a second or third time gave me hope and clarity when I felt stuck.

There's another aspect of this engaging pursuit I want to make clear: I don't pretend to be an expert interpreter of *A Course in Miracles*.® I am a student, like you, nothing more. My commitment to the *Course* as a practical way of life is avid. And it has been my personal practice for many years to write meditations that reflect and, I hope, enlighten me about the spiritual journey that has become my life. This ongoing activity defines who I am, and sharing these reflections with others through the written word seems to be my calling. That desire, and nothing more, gave rise to the daily meditations here. It has been my way to better use the *Course* teachings. My simple hope is that they will help you too.

In a Twelve Step program I've attended for many years we have a saying that goes like this: *Take what fits and leave the rest.* That's my humble suggestion to you in regard to these meditations. Some may be easily grasped and immediately helpful as you move through the day's activities. Some may not fit you currently. That's okay. When they don't, let them go. Don't let the ego kick up a fuss regarding them. My intent has been only to help, first myself and then you, to practically apply what the *Course* speaks of. My own understanding of *A Course in Miracles*® changes and deepens daily. Obviously this means that were I to write another edition of *Daily Meditations for Practicing the Course,* it would be different and, I hope, closer to the purity of the *Course's* message. Each of us gains clarity all the time. That's the good news.

I wish you well on your journey. We are lucky people to have found this pathway. Every experience we have had or will ever have can look differently to us now. The miracles have only just begun.

JANUARY

We are exactly where we need to be right now.

It's good to be reminded that we are where we need to be, particularly if we're prone to think we are missing out on some opportunity or fearful that we aren't making significant progress in our careers or other areas. When we doubt that we're doing enough in any regard, this principle helps us quiet down and ready ourselves to peacefully do the next thing. It will always surface.

It's comforting to realize there are no accidents, no coincidences happening in our lives. What we need to experience, to learn, to teach, in order to complete our journey home, will spring forth when the timing is perfect. We'll never have to search in vain for our next assignment. It will capture our attention.

There is never a need for lamentations. If we haven't fulfilled some task to our satisfaction, we can redo it. Now. If we haven't treated a companion or co-worker respectfully, we can make amends. Now. There isn't anything complicated about how to move through this day or these activities. We simply need to walk with the Holy Spirit and we'll get to our destination on time.

There are no mistakes in what comes my way today. How I respond depends on who I ask to help me see the circumstances.

Problems

The Holy Spirit makes all things possible.

Nearly every day we are overwhelmed, at least once, by a situation, an assignment, or an individual. Momentarily we are certain we can't handle what we're called on to do. As new students of the *Course,* we often revert back to old behavior and start an argument as a way of diverting attention from the inadequacy we feel. That behavior never solves anything and it nearly always initiates a counterattack. Then disorder reigns.

Now we know there is another way to live. We don't always choose it and our pain is our evidence. But it's never too late to reject a familiar, unsuccessful approach, even while in the midst of the experience. Nothing remains daunting if tackled with the help of the Holy Spirit. The Holy Spirit sees only peace within the turmoil of experiences. We'll be able to see only peace too. Let's waste no more time in chaos!

Nothing is too big or hard or confusing for me to handle today if I seek the Holy Spirit's help.

Miracles result from a shift in our perceptions.

Every expression is either one of love or a cry for healing and help. Remembering this simplifies how we experience life. The most difficult of circumstances reveals a far simpler lesson than we might imagine when it is perceived through loving eyes and a forgiving heart.

But what of the abuse, physical or emotional, we may have suffered at the hands of parents or spouses? Can those experiences be forgotten, forgiven, or simply explained away? *A Course in Miracles*® teaches us that every unloving action is always a cry for healing and help. Regardless of its intensity, an act that hurts us is a cry for help that has grown out of fear.

Embracing this truth doesn't come easily at first. Maybe we can accept it in a few situations. A friend's put-down or the bus driver's rude remark can be overlooked. But the more serious circumstances require our willingness to suspend all judgment and offer only forgiveness instead. With time and practice this will become easier.

I will quietly think through an action before I take it today.
I will ask myself, Is this action loving?

Insight
Inadequacy

Take what fits and leave the rest.

Perhaps because we are in pain, we want to understand *A Course in Miracles*® immediately, certain that we'll be instantly healed. The truth is, we will likely move slowly through the text and the workbook and still miss many finer points of the message. In time, all will become clear.

Just because we don't understand every statement Jesus makes in the *Course* doesn't mean we can't immediately incorporate those we do understand. For instance, it's easy to grasp that fear results in attack or to accept that love is fear's opposite. Thus, we can quickly evaluate any person's action as either an expression of love or an appeal for healing and help. Knowing just this one principle can change how we see every situation in our lives. Grasping the rest will eventually change us forever. There is enough time for understanding all of it.

I will apply what I have learned so far today.
That's easy enough.

The ego will lead me astray.

When we first come to *A Course in Miracles*,® we are baffled by the idea that the ego is like a "problem child." Surely, letting the ego guide us can't hurt us! But ever so gently, we learn it may. Simultaneously, we also learn that we are served far more advantageously by the Holy Spirit. While this may not upset us, we don't know how to access the Holy Spirit initially. If we're in a study group, we can learn how together.

What does it mean to be guided by the Holy Spirit? Every person discovers the Inner Voice a bit differently, but we all do access It in the quiet spaces of our minds. For everyone, the basic element is the same. We call it love. Looking at our experiences, our friends, our casual acquaintances, even our enemies, through eyes that see only love, initiates in us a far different response than when the ego asserts control. We have no thought of attack or comparison or conflict when love is our guide.

Looking with love on the first person I meet today will help me look with love at the second and third one too.

Letting go

Let's guard against planning the day.

It's not easy to *let things happen* without our direction. Parents and other educators taught us that the better organized we are, the more we anticipate the behavior of others and plan our reaction, the greater our success will be. What they didn't say was that we have two inner voices available for guidance: the ego's and the Holy Spirit's. The quieter voice is recognized too seldom, thus chaos often reigns.

Because we mistakenly think the situations we encounter have inherent meaning, we get fearful about managing them correctly. The easier route, simply stepping aside and letting experiences unfold as they will, seems irresponsible.

We can change our course of action midstream. That's the good news. The ego's suggestions seldom lead to happy endings. If we want these, we need to be willing to get quiet and listen to the other voice that speaks to us.

If I start making detailed plans for myself or others today,
I'll be frustrated or angry soon.
There is another way.

Oneness

Nothing exists beyond me to make me fearful.

The ego is so easily threatened and so intent on keeping us under its control. It conjures up adversaries for us to battle, maintaining its control over our perspective and feelings. It doesn't matter that the attacker would disappear if we turned our attention to the Holy Spirit. In the heat of the confrontation, the ego is in charge and that means we can't even imagine the presence of the Holy Spirit.

Our problem is figuring out how to get beyond this belief system. It's really far simpler than we'd imagined. It requires only a little willingness to understand our existence differently. Hope opens the door to the Holy Spirit, and It will always show us our connection, not separation from others. We'll get the glimmers we need of the Oneness that is truth if we really seek them.

I am not separate from anyone today.
We are in union; we complete
one another.

Guilt is most often unconscious.

If our guilt is unconscious, how can we deal with it? The surprising news for many of us is that every unloving encounter with someone else is an opportunity to deal with guilt. What this means is that we see ourselves in others. Always. Other people serve as our mirrors. While it is more pleasant to relate to others' positive behavior, we can learn a lot about ourselves from our reactions to their negative behaviors.

The *Course* invites us to forgive others. In the process we'll discover a self-love we hadn't known before. The guilt we carry is usually deep-seated. While it's true we are conscious of our grossly "sinful" acts, the more subtle we fail to perceive. That's why we encounter them as traits in our companions. They teach us about ourselves. Forgiving them allows us to forgive ourselves and heal our minds. From that moment on, nothing remains the same.

I will heal my mind by forgiving others today.
I can do it again tomorrow if necessary.

We are both teachers and students.

Our problems frequently arise because we resist relying on the Holy Spirit to interpret our experiences. The conflicts that snag us seem quite real when we forget our true selves. How can we return to more peaceful times? By changing our minds.

It's a powerful realization to know that we can be as peaceful as we make up our minds to be. The years of agonizing over how we should react to unloving experiences can be gone forever. It doesn't matter what "he said" or what "she did." Any action that isn't loving is simply a fearful call for healing and help.

Throughout each day we are given many opportunities to act as Teachers to our fellow companions. Anytime we forget to look to the Holy Spirit for guidance, a fellow teacher will remind us. We are always Teacher or student, one or the other. There is no shame in forgetting how to teach. Our understanding will grow with each passing experience.

I will take a moment to remember
who the real Teacher is today.
And I will listen to the lesson.

Illness
Unforgiveness

 Unforgiveness makes us sick.

For many of us it's hard to understand that a dear friend suffering from a terminal illness has been made sick by her unforgiveness. She may not even seem angry or resentful, perhaps. Yet the *Course* tells us that hanging on to past hurts hinders our present health. Could her acknowledgment of this and willingness to forgive make her well?

Forgiveness might not erase the physical ailment, but her mental state would reflect a more loving attitude, which is where one's actual "wellness" lies. The body embraces what the mind projects. Fully understanding this principle gives us the capacity to create *miraculous* lives.

When we have a headache or suffer from indigestion, we are quick to look outside for the cause. While the external environment may be harsh and demanding, it can't make us sick. It doesn't determine our attitude. Taking responsibility for who we are is the most healing action we can take.

Am I hanging on to an old hurt?
The condition of my body may give
me a clue today.

*Mistakes are merely teaching
and learning opportunities.*

When the shame and guilt we cultivate because of our errors create more mistakes they gain momentum. Instead of growing from our mistakes, we let them diminish us. And so our relationships with others are likewise diminished.

We can instantly halt the momentum, however. That's the promise Jesus has made us. But how do we do it? The decision to look upon every circumstance through the loving eyes of the inner Spirit helps us resist the knee-jerk response we've grown accustomed to making. Until we experiment with this change, we can't imagine the results.

The holy Inner Voice has only soft, understanding words to offer in even the most difficult of times. Being soothed through the minefield makes us appreciate the opportunities we have for listening anew.

*I will look upon my struggles today
as opportunities to hear
the Holy Spirit's message.*

January 12

Worries

Taking my worries to the "light"
lets me relinquish them.

Coming to fully appreciate how much simpler our lives can be doesn't happen overnight. Most of us spent years living in the turmoil of the ego. Every fight seemed justified to us. It was important to be right! Choosing peacefulness rather than winning an argument made us feel weak, not peaceful.

How differently we look at the rifts that disturb each day now. We see problems as opportunities to express the Holy Spirit's love. Never before have we felt so empowered, so in control of our lives. We could not have imagined before beginning this course of study that life could feel so free of pain and struggle.

Fulfilling our destiny is now much simpler. We will discover what to do next if we bring the situation to the "light" of our inner understanding. That's where the Holy Spirit resides. All "right" responses will be revealed to us there.

Today lies before me uncluttered by the ego.
I will keep the turmoil at bay.
The Holy Spirit is my guide.

*God's voice is present
even when we're not listening.*

It's beneficial to know that God never leaves our side. Obviously we don't always listen to His guidance. And even when we do, we neglect to follow it sometimes. If we followed it, we'd experience every situation in our lives far more peacefully. However, recognizing God's presence even once is a beginning. Any change we make in this regard strengthens our willingness to listen to God more quickly the next time we're feeling indecisive.

What keeps us from listening to the words of God? For most of us, the interloper is the incessantly nagging ego. It drowns out the Holy Spirit. Unfortunately, we're never benefited by the ego's suggestions, but it keeps us too busy to evaluate our actions. We mistake busyness for worthiness, perhaps. Let's remember we are always worthy in God's eyes. It's the ego that labels us unworthy.

We'd be so much happier, so much more peaceful, if we gave our total attention to the Holy Spirit. Can that be so hard?

*Today's activities will trip me many times unless I keep my mind
on God. Any discomfort I have is my clue my mind
has wandered.*

January 14

Ego

By ourselves, we can do nothing.

Let's celebrate rather than lament our need to ask the Holy Spirit for help. Relying on that source of power eases every encounter we'll have today. Of course, the ego wants to handle all situations alone. The ego cries for self-sufficiency; however, our greatest problems result from the ego's control. The ego is always out to protect itself, at the expense of all else.

In time we will come to believe that the only thing we need to do, ever, is to be forgiving. We got our training for life from parents or friends who suffered from an overly active ego too. Letting go of our ego-driven responses may seem irresponsible. Giving only love to the people and the experiences we're having may feel different from how we interacted in the past. Letting the Holy Spirit take charge of our lives gives us peace and simplifies the activities of every day. We can stop manipulating and judging others if we rely on the Holy Spirit for all things.

Through the Holy Spirit all questions are answered today.
All plans are complete.

Asking for what we really want is necessary.

It's important to ask for what we really want, because our lives will reflect that which we dwell on. What we dwell on may bring us only pain unless we are specific and intent on the opposite. When looked at this way, we discover that life is not nearly as mysterious as we might have imagined. This doesn't make it any less interesting, however. Only more peaceful.

How do we know what we really want? Perhaps that's our main point of confusion. But looking inward we'll find the answer we deserve. That's where the Holy Spirit resides. Our safety and happiness are assured if we let that quiet voice direct us. How can we be sure that's the voice we hear? By evaluating the message. Is it one of love? If not, getting quiet again is the best, next step.

I may not be certain what I want today, but the Holy Spirit's voice will clarify it for me. My task is to ask.

Separation
Peace

 The separation we feel from others is not real.

All tension and conflict with other people are the result of our perceptions. Coming to understand that situations appear as we project them changes how we feel. What we perceive as being external is created by us internally. The mind is all-powerful.

How can it be that nothing exists but what we make up? Objects feel concrete when touched. So do people. Yet the *Course* tells us that in a tiny, mad moment we made it all up. In that moment, we imagined our separation from God, and existence became a struggle to get back to where we began, to escape this nightmare called life.

We have to accept many theories—whether scientific or religious—on faith. This is one of them. And until we do, we can at least envision that the mind consists of two parts. One is the ego, which manifests itself as problems. The other is the Holy Spirit, where peace dwells. We listen to the voice of one part or the other every minute. We can choose only peace if we listen to the Holy Spirit.

The voice that blesses me is as close as my memory of its presence.
I will select carefully today.

*Whatever happens can be
interpreted for our good.*

When disaster seems to strike, it's hard to understand that whatever happens is for our good. It helps to understand that our perception judged the situation a disaster. By changing one's perception, we can change the effects of an experience. What looked bad one minute may be seen as quite fortuitous the next. Asking the Holy Spirit for a better or different understanding of a circumstance can offer us a dramatically different experience.

How we choose to see our experiences and the people who share them with us is at our discretion. While it's true that we don't have the power to control much, we do have authority over how we view the details of our lives. Of course, this assures us that we'll be as content and peaceful as we want to be. Or just the opposite. At a moment's notice, we can be transformed. That's a thrilling opportunity. Our transformation can positively affect all those who share our journey.

*I will be blessed with all the right experiences today.
I can maximize them for my good.*

Healing
Oneness

To join with others is to heal.

We get together with others all the time. We join them for dinner, for movies, for cards, for conversation, for intimacy. But coming together with someone for a single purposeful encounter is not the same as *joining with* them. How it differs is the key lesson we're here to learn.

Joining, as defined by the *Course,* means understanding our singleness of real purpose here. It means remembering the One Spirit that resides in all of us. It's about honoring each other as the sole creation of God. It's about pure love.

When we are not remembering our Oneness, not remembering to love, we are feeling the fear of separateness, of comparison, of conflict, of competition, of judgment, of lack. We are not at peace. We are not in the presence of the Holy Spirit. We are not healed. But it is never too late to learn the lesson of Oneness, of forgiveness, and thus of healing. The other people on our path are our vehicles for the journey.

*If I want healing today, healing of the mind or body, I need
only remember the holy place within where
the Holy Spirit resides.*

We teach and learn interchangeably.

We'll have a number of opportunities every day to inspire peaceful resolutions to problems. That may sound unlikely or grandiose if we haven't considered the impact the Holy Spirit can have on the lives of everyone. Our changed perspective of any situation can nurture extremely unexpected outcomes.

What a thrill it is to realize that we can offer something good to every situation, every person we encounter. When we rely on the Holy Spirit to dictate our offering, it can only be good.

What we are teaching someone else in these moments is the possibility that love is forever present in our lives. Even when we feel distant from love, we can claim it by seeking the closeness of the Holy Spirit.

We learn from others' behavior. We teach them likewise. It is up to us to decide what we want to teach and learn in every instance. The ego has a particular plan for us. So does the Holy Spirit. Choosing one plan or the other makes the difference in how quickly we will "graduate."

I am a willing student when I want to be. Will I be a willing Teacher today?

Peace

Seek peacefulness.

Few of us would admit to wanting anything but peace. Why then does it evade us so often? We hear repeatedly that we receive that which we seek. Do we not seek peace? Obviously we do not. What we think we want and what we obsess about are frequently far different. The latter is what we get.

The formula for discovering peace is simple. Try the following: Stop thinking. Get quiet. Turn your attention to the Spirit within and ask for clarity, for a different perspective, for a forgiving heart. *Peace will come.*

If it's so easy, why aren't we surrounded by more peaceful companions? Because the noisy ego is so seductive. It clamors for our attention just as it clamors for control of our lives and the lives of others. The ego convinces us we'll be more secure if it's in charge. Painfully learning, again and again, that that's not the case eventually leaves an indelible mark. Peace will seek us then.

My journey will enlighten me today if I'm attentive.

A call for healing and help is easily recognized.

Any behavior we observe or are the brunt of can be classified instantly. It is either the reflection of a loving thought or an appeal for help and healing. Depending on its nature, the behavior triggers in us a response. Too often it will be ill-conceived. If we haven't consulted with the Holy Spirit first, we're letting the ego dictate our response, and the outcome benefits no one.

Isn't there a way to control our behavior? Certainly. And it's not a mystery known only to a few. We have been apprised of the presence of the Holy Spirit within our minds, but we may not have accessed it often. That's not unusual or something to be ashamed of. We're still learning. But we do need to acknowledge the truth of it, and then seek the Spirit's involvement in the preparation of all responses from this moment forth. When we do, no appeal for healing and help will be met with anger or worse.

*I can be certain I'll hurt no one today if I consult
with the Holy Spirit before taking action.*

Right Mind

 *All attack thoughts are gone when we
are in our Right Mind.*

We complicate our lives. We analyze, make judgments, argue, and feel either superior or inferior to others. The mind we nourish is seldom quiet; it's generally agitated, and we don't even realize the peace we're missing.

Where is the Right Mind the *Course* speaks of if we're not automatically in it? This sounds so mysterious, doesn't it? We are learning that we have two minds: one is in the ego's camp and one is nurtured by the Holy Spirit. Whichever one we turn to moment by moment decides the tenor of the experience we'll have. Discovering, as we eventually do, that we are *always* peaceful in one mind and *always* agitated in the other, makes the best choice obvious.

*I will be peaceful regardless of what is happening today
if I stay Right-Minded.*

*The Holy Spirit needs little from us
to change our lives.*

Living in a world of conflict and confusion is familiar to all of us. Far too many conversations end in disagreement. Often we or someone else reneges on plans that aren't unfolding in the right way. Many people in our lives aren't fun, or at least not with us, nor are they supportive of our efforts at living. In all of these, and in many other instances, the "problems" that trouble us seem to be *out there*. Someone else isn't doing *something* right or the conflict and tension would not be present. What's the solution?

We've acquired some helpful information about addressing these kinds of situations from the *Course*. Just as was true for the scribes of the *Course*, we'll be shown another way to experience every detail of our lives if that's truly our desire. Being willing to want a better way, then being willing to ask for one, promises us that we'll be shown one when the time is right. Our lives will not resemble what they were when we make this tiny adjustment in what we want and what we do.

*If I'm just a bit willing to see an experience
differently today, it will change.
Pronto!*

Peace
Choice

To know peace is the miracle.

How often do we awaken anxious about the details of the next twenty-four hours? Perhaps a simple phone call from a friend jars us from the serenity we nurtured during meditation. Or the journey to work may have started out smoothly enough, but a traffic jam changed all that. Maintaining a peaceful perspective is difficult. Can *A Course in Miracles*® really make a difference in our lives?

The *Course* doesn't claim to eradicate the turmoil in our lives. Nor does it control our actions or beliefs in any way. The journey we chart and the experiences we have are of our own volition. How we feel about them, how we use them, how we incorporate them into our lives is up to us. However, there is always another way to see whatever we have created, and that's the gift the *Course* offers us. The mere request, "Show me another vision of what's happening now," invites the Holy Spirit to interpret the details of the moment. Feeling peace in the midst of the devastation is possible. Always.

No circumstance will overwhelm me today
if I ask to see a different picture.

*Our desire to understand anything
is the first important step.*

There are numerous elements in the *Course*'s teachings that baffle us. When we're informed that *this world we think we see* is not real confusion sets in big time. What is *this* that we see? The world outside of us mirrors the world we think we want to see; we project it. In the process, we project the people we see too. The key element here is who we put in charge of the projection: the ego or the Holy Spirit. If the ego is relied on, we'll see conflict and pain. If the Holy Spirit speaks, we'll know forgiveness and love.

It's not beyond us to have total understanding of this process. The real gift is that we'll have exactly the world of experiences we really deserve when we seek the Spirit's view.

*I can live in darkness today or I can take the mysteries
to the light of the Holy Spirit. My understanding
of this life will grow.*

Forgiveness

 Let's forgive ourselves for the world we've created.

Within moments of arising each day, we must assume responsibility for the circumstances that unfold. That which we see and experience is not real; however, we have created it as such and then reacted to it. How can we avoid this? Many of us feel at a loss to live differently, primarily because we don't realize what we are doing each moment. We have forgotten we are living a dream.

Are we willing to accept this as true, that we are wholly responsible for the ills we observe in this world? There is a way to do it with the help of the *Course,* and that's by forgiving ourselves for the mistakes we make. The Holy Spirit is eager to show us how.

We aren't evil people; the ego has simply distorted our vision. With the Holy Spirit's help, we'll be shown what is actually real. The blessing in this is we grow in our ability to forgive everyone else too. We are, afterall, One. What another seemingly has done is only the mistake we, ourselves, have made.

Forgiveness is the only lesson we need to learn.
By asking the Holy Spirit for help today,
I will be shown how to forgive.

Scarcity

The scarcity principle governs too many lives.

We lack nothing. We certainly don't think that and we don't live as though that's true, but, in fact, we are perfect, whole in every way, loved totally by our Creator, equal to everyone we see. Unfortunately, we don't see ourselves through God's eyes so we assume we are flawed, inadequate, not worthy of the love we crave from others.

How dark we have made this world we see. At times, we wonder if it will ever change, if we will ever change. At those times, let's look closer at the friends we admire. Perhaps they see a sunnier side of life. It's important that we understand we have the same capabilities as everyone else. We are everyone else! To see a lighter side of something, we need only ask for another view. By carrying our dark perception to the light, to the Holy Spirit, we'll garner another vision. The rapidity with which we do this defines how long our world looks dark.

I lack nothing today. The Holy Spirit guarantees me guidance and safety and love.

Inadequacy

The ego creates the notion of lack.

Being told we are perfect, that we lack nothing at all, seems unfathomable. We have nervously sought help because we feel so imperfect, so inadequate. Surely there is something wrong with us. Our plea is that this *Course* will cure us.

The readings and the discussions in the *Course* introduce us to ideas that will heal us, but not in the way we'd imagined. We are relieved to learn that our own split mind has caused our perpetual discomfort, that what we feel and see when we think we're lacking is not the real us. But how can we be somebody else and still feel like this?

We're lucky to have companions who remind us to be patient. The understanding we crave will come to us. For now, it's enough to grasp that the ego creates our inadequacy, and it survives only because we listen to it. Our assignment is to turn a deaf ear to the ego.

I am not imperfect in any way.
I will ignore the ego today.

The spirit, not the body, is what's real.

Everything that we look at and touch affirms that our bodies are real. We check the mirror each morning and see our reflection. We do push-ups and leg lifts to tighten and strengthen our muscles. We bump an elbow and screech in pain. Department stores attract us like magnets with the latest fashions to adorn our bodies. Yet the *Course* teaches us that our bodies aren't real!

Anybody who has ever had a blister, a broken arm, a sprained ankle resists the information that the body isn't real. The pain certainly felt real enough. Perhaps it's easier to take on faith that our bodies are vehicles for learning. Outside our minds, our bodies don't exist. That still isn't easy to grasp, unconditionally, but we may have discovered in *Course* groups that others have come to believe it. For now, let's just follow their example.

Some things I will have to accept on faith for a time.
Making the decision to do so is the only hard part.

Ego

The ego lives to attack.

As students of the *Course,* we realize how frequently the ego takes charge of our thinking and our actions. Our first response to a multitude of situations is to attack. Backed-up traffic, mean-spirited neighbors, an overly demanding boss—all easily trigger our ire. We observe many fellow travelers reacting in much the same way. We wonder, can it ever be different?

Fortunately, we have all met people on our journey, perhaps through the *Course* or even on the bus, who appear to face all of life's experiences with a smile. How do they do it? We may never figure them out, but they have served to teach us of the possibility that there is another way.

We are here, now, because we want the "other" way. We can learn to accept that the ego is not, nor ever was, our friend. It will injure our relationships, hinder our health, destroy or distort our dreams. We didn't learn this lesson in school or at home. We can learn it now, however. We'll smile more easily when we do.

I will give the ego a rest today.
I will flow with my experiences.

The body is used by the ego or
the Holy Spirit to communicate.

We say the body isn't real and then we proceed to affect it by the mind. How can this be? What we mean when we say the body isn't real is that it reflects what the mind projects. It doesn't exist independently. It has no intrinsic, unchanging properties. It does communicate quite emphatically and prolifically, however. And that's because the mind, from either the Holy Spirit's perspective or the ego's, is communicating through the body all the time.

How might we see this from a practical standpoint? We can all recognize when someone (some *body*) physically attacks another body. What has occurred is that the ego has made a suggestion to the mind that the body fulfilled. The body didn't devise this action. It does only what it's told to do.

On the other hand, when we note someone smiling and looking beyond an attack statement, we can be certain the Holy Spirit is acting. We are never at a loss to understand the cause of another's behavior. We must see ours likewise.

My body reveals who is doing my thinking.
Today's experiences will unfold accordingly.

FEBRUARY

Miracles can happen on a regular basis.

We may often say, "I could sure use a miracle." How many times a day do we wish for something different to be happening? We want the miracle of winning the lottery, perhaps. Or the miracle of the perfect spouse or job or boss. Waking up with a different body would seem like a miracle to many of us. So would developing the perfect golf swing. The actual miracle is that we can have any of these. We can have all of them, in fact. But how?

We learn from the *Course* that miracles are as plentiful as we make up our minds they are. What brings them about is our willingness to change how we perceive the job, the boss, the body, the golf game. Miracles reside within our minds. They always have. The wonderful part is that we can have as many miracles as we truly desire.

If a situation is bothering us, could it be that there's a different way to see it? We'll discover, just as quickly as we try, that nothing looks the same once we ask that question and free our minds for the real answer.

I can have as many miracles as I want today. Feeling only love and joy is possible if I change my mind.

Action
Unity

 I am not separate from others. I only think I am.

It seems foreign to think of ourselves as One with others. How can we see others unless they are separate from us? Many of the lessons of the *Course* require faith. In time, we will recognize the truth of these lessons. We will also learn we can live in this world with ease.

We need to remember that whatever we do to others we do to ourselves. If I snap at you, I get stung. If I gossip about you, I feel untrustworthy. If I hit you, I injure my own sense of self. Everything I do boomerangs back to me.

The concept of our connectedness is elusive. Probably the best way to grasp the idea is by noticing exactly how we feel each time we interact with other people. However we receive them, we receive ourselves. By loving them, we feel loved. By honoring them, we feel honored. By forgiving them, we become forgiven.

Today I will treat others as I want to be treated.
After all, we are One and the same.

The Real World is not what I see.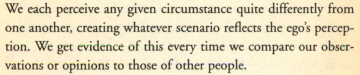

We each perceive any given circumstance quite differently from one another, creating whatever scenario reflects the ego's perception. We get evidence of this every time we compare our observations or opinions to those of other people.

The obvious question is, if what any of us see is not the Real World, where is it? Because we are experiencing life in *these* bodies, with *these* companions, we may feel unwilling to accept that only our minds are real. We think we need to see and touch something concrete to accept it as real.

Let's remember that what we see is what we need to see, for now, that is. We are students on a journey "home," where we'll no longer feel separate from God. Occasionally, we are overcome by a feeling of peacefulness, particularly when we remember this. The quiet mind is where peace resides. We can go there as often as we'd like.

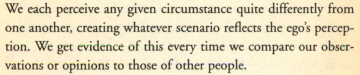

The Holy Mind is real.
All else the ego makes up.

Forgiveness

 The act of forgiving reverses how we think.

No matter what we may pretend, we feel guilty and ashamed. We don't have to recognize this for it to be true. Some ideas ultimately have to be accepted. Our *Course* Teachers have no doubt learned this already. Now our turn has come. The test of its truth lies in how we perceive the many people in our lives. Do we feel judgmental or maybe fearful? Probably so. Our guilt is secure. What comes next?

What we have to do is recognize that our judgment is really against ourselves. We put it out there because we don't want to claim it. When we acknowledge this, however, our feelings begin to change. Compassion replaces judgment. We are changed, thus everyone in our world is changed when we see correctly the truth of our own guilt.

We need not stay guilty. It doesn't serve us. We didn't earn it either. We created it just as we created this insane world. We can quit responding to it with a small change of mind. Nothing is stopping us but the ego.

Do I like myself today? If I have any doubts,
I'm judging myself unfairly. I can give this up!

The Holy Spirit is always present.

We can always count on the Holy Spirit to direct our thoughts and actions. However, we must be vigilant about asking for this guidance. We need to remember that the ego wants to be our director too. How do we know which "voice" we are listening to? The answer is always the same. If the act we are about to take or the words we are about to say are not purely loving, we aren't attuned to the Holy Spirit. It's just that simple.

Each day we are bombarded by opportunities to interact with other people who help us get in touch with our spiritual needs. Even the most difficult relationships offer us opportunities to grow and heal. Every person around us helps us return "home" to the realm of the Holy Spirit. In that realm, there is only love, nothing more. Our companions here, now, are the links to the realm of love.

*I can have constant contact with the Holy Spirit if
I am aware of the ego's attempts to control me.*

February 6

Insanity

 Insanity or peacefulness, that's the choice.

This choice seems too simplistic, perhaps. How can we go from being peaceful to insane so quickly? Few of us had little more than a hint of understanding about this when we first sought the counsel of the *Course*. Our minds madly tried to solve or change or merely tolerate the circumstances we were living our whole lives. We frequently felt out of control, insane so to speak. And that seemed normal.

We learn now that it could have been different all along. We hear in the voices and see in the actions of our *Course* friends that it is different for some of them. We wonder why they have been graced and not us. Our time has come, however.

Each passage we read, each discussion we hear, each interpretation we seek enlightens us about the pathway to the realm of peacefulness. We, too, can know only peace. Are we ready?

I may be enticed by the ego today.
Will I choose peace instead?

Love

What is not love is always fear.

We don't always interpret fear quickly. That's because it wears many faces. Violent rage seldom looks like fear to us. Neither does a bully's humiliation of a school chum. Tearful pleading may be recognized as fear, but only because it doesn't threaten us. Is every act that is not love fear? We may have to remind ourselves often that it is.

Daily we'll observe many instances of fear. The action called for from us is compassion. In the expression of it, we'll reap its benefit. In the same way that fear fosters more fear if not met with love, compassion also multiplies. Being a purveyor of the latter helps to heal all who enter our realm today.

Perhaps we think we can always recognize love, but is that true? Let's expand our horizons. Love may be silence. It may be laughter or tears. It may be unexpected agreement from an adversary. Love will never be hostile, but it may be subtle.

I will look for signs of love today. I will express them whether I see them or not.

Problems

Problems are manufactured by the ego.

When we're in conflict with a friend or even a stranger, we must remember that no tension would exist if we hadn't created it. Taking full responsibility for whatever we're experiencing isn't easy to do. It's so much easier to blame the other person for our troubles. Being told, as we are in the *Course*, that problems are always created by the ego is both alarming and confusing.

How do we get from where we are to being able to fully embrace that idea? Surely not by resisting it. Nor arguing about it. Some things we just have to take on faith. This is one of those things. But how do we begin changing how our minds seem to work? We simply and sincerely ask the Holy Spirit for help, and then we get quiet. It's not as difficult as it seems. It takes willingness, lots of practice, and very little more.

Our problems might even be seen as the ego's desire for us to seek spiritual help. At this stage of our growth we're seldom inclined to do so without the push. But the time will come when we'll need no more pushing. This is perhaps the greatest miracle we'll realize.

*The ego mind leads me astray. Today I'll remember
my journey is about changing my mind.*

Hate

Changing hate to love is possible.

If our memories are filled with pain, we may find it hard to let go of the hate we feel is justified. Being told our parents did the best they could maybe doesn't agree with us all that well. Transgressions against us now are just as difficult to overlook. And we wonder if it's right to relieve others of responsibility for their behavior. Many psychologies and philosophies suggest we shouldn't. But where does that get us? That's the burning question.

Blaming others for our problems denies the individual journey we are each here to make. While we may agree that no one in his or her Right Mind wants to experience pain and trauma, most of us don't live in our Right Mind all that often. The Right Mind is the one that knows and sees only love. From its perspective, there have been no injuries or transgressions. What we saw and felt was what the ego sought. Nothing less.

Living in our Right Mind is the only way to change our hate to love. Living in our Right Mind, we acknowledge that our journey has been purposeful and we have learned the glory of love.

*If I feel hate or anger today, I'll recognize it
as an opportunity to "change my mind."*

Guidance

 The Holy Spirit is at our beck and call.

All our good acts are aided by the Holy Spirit. We may not have known this consciously; thus seeking Its help moment by moment didn't occur to us. But now we know. The Holy Spirit does not reside in some far-off place. We carry It within and It awaits our call.

Intentionally turning to It for help is all the action we need to take to change the course of events in our lives. Disasters are averted when we respond according to the Holy Spirit. Testing this thesis may be necessary for some of us. That's okay. Learning by doing is positive action.

We will have innumerable opportunities today to ask the Holy Spirit for help. Going to this Source again and again for direction and discovering the peace inherent in the action make belief in Its value unquestionable. What a gift it is knowing how to remedy any tension in our lives, great or small.

Today I will consult the Holy Voice within before I act.

Our relationships always reflect our state of mind.

Sometimes we feel hurt and angry at everyone. It seems as if the world is out to get us. At these times, it's well to remember that our attitudes deeply influence how we see the world and the people around us. We can remember to "turn the other cheek." When we meet an affront with kindness, the perpetrator miraculously backs off. The lesson is not that elusive.

We frequently lament the characteristics of our relationships. There is not enough intimacy, there is too much disagreement, or we share too few interests. Perhaps we have too few friends. The solution to our relationship problems is to check out our inner perceptions. The signals we send to others define what we get back in return.

When we meet happy people, we'll likely soon see the balance in their lives, the level of peace in their relationships. Positive attitudes and healthy relationships go hand in hand. Fortunately, we're in charge of the attitudes we nurture.

I am seeking the hand of the Holy Spirit today.
The joy is mine.

Salvation

 Salvation of the world is our task.

There is so much we fail to understand or handle perfectly each day, it seems, that we can't imagine how or why we're assigned to save the world. When understood in the principles of *A Course in Miracles,*® we realize we can do whatever is expected of us. But let's review how this happens.

All the different physical bodies present in this illusory world are here for the same reason. The ego split off from God in an instant of madness and made up this experience. Forever after, we have sought to blame one another for all the problems endured, always believing that if others would only do our will, all conflict would subside. But that's not salvation, and salvation is our task. Conflicts offer the path to salvation, however.

When a conflict occurs, recognize it as an invitation to look but not really see. The process of not seeing it allows us to feel and appreciate a moment of peace rather than tension, and others are lovingly affected by our forgiving approach to conflict. Our contribution toward salvation is being made in this instance.

If problems seem too big for me today, perhaps I have not sought the guidance of the Holy Spirit.

The world "outside" is only a projection of the ego.

Newspapers bombard us with examples of violence and pain. Magazines succeed in increasing their circulation when they hype stories of the bizarre or perverted elements of society. Movies that glorify murder always have an audience. Can it be true that we have made up all of this madness?

It's not easy to understand that nothing outside of our minds is real. It certainly seems as if the news we hear and read about is happening. And on one level it is—the level of the ego. But the purpose of the "madness" is to finally bring us back to the other part of our minds—the part we call holy. When we choose that space, we are at peace. In that space we don't see or hear the madness. In that space we are secure, filled with love, and free from the stories that haunt us.

The world we project may mystify us. Why would we seek pain, or worse? How we learn our lessons has been up to us. That we learn the main one is all that really matters.

Today I will see only love. All else will fall away before my eyes.

February 14

Special relationships

 A special relationship will not satisfy us.

The greeting card industry hails the value of "specialness." When we were youngsters we longed to be told we were special. It meant we stood out from the crowd. We wanted that distinction. Now we are seeing how standing out engenders separation and comparisons. As a result, we fear not being equal.

A special relationship, then, is one where we note differences, where we vie for control. We see friend or partner as a separate mind and a separate body we should mold to ensure that our own wishes are fulfilled. Any deviation from our expectations is reason for conflict. Life, therefore, becomes perpetual conflict in the realm of specialness.

The holy relationship beckons as we grow in the *Course*. Our vision will change. We will not seek control. We'll acknowledge our oneness; we'll value our sameness with others. We'll gradually know love, and nothing will look the same.

Seeing a friend or a partner through holy eyes today changes who we both are.

Change the mind and the behavior follows.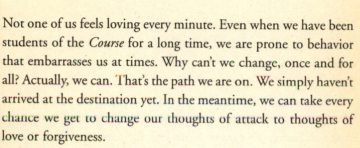

Not one of us feels loving every minute. Even when we have been students of the *Course* for a long time, we are prone to behavior that embarrasses us at times. Why can't we change, once and for all? Actually, we can. That's the path we are on. We simply haven't arrived at the destination yet. In the meantime, we can take every chance we get to change our thoughts of attack to thoughts of love or forgiveness.

In some situations, it seems easier to change our behavior than our minds. For instance, when arguing with a friend, we may be certain we are right. But we don't have to yell or pout. We may keep our opinion, in fact, and our friends can keep theirs. It doesn't matter really. And that's what we come to understand. None of these differences really matter. They are nothing more than vehicles for learning what is real, what is important.

The quiet mind knows the only truth that matters. We will visit that place more frequently now. Our behavior will signal the change in us.

I may hope to change someone else by my actions today.
That's folly. All I can change is my mind and
my desire to change other people.

Problems
Blame

We can heal all our problems.

We love to blame others for what ails us. Yet this is never satisfying for long. It's much more fruitful to accept responsibility for whatever is going on in our lives, because only then can we get free of the problem for good.

This seems impossible, perhaps. But until we have taken charge of the perspective we desire, we can't fathom how easy it really is. Seeing the events of our lives through the loving eyes of the Holy Spirit eliminates their sting. What we perceive as problems are nothing more than faulty perceptions of the myriad expressions of love or appeals for healing and help. Cultivating the willingness and vision to see only love are wonderful exercises for the mind.

Problems are as fleeting as the blink of my eye.
They can also be refocused on at will.
I am the healer of my life.

Only God knows what's best for us.

"I don't know. Only God knows." We often utter these words, but seldom do we deliberate their meaning. The truth of it, however, is awesome indeed. And we can tap into this realm by merely seeking to hear the voice of God. Most of the hassle in our lives would dissipate, leaving no trace, if we actually sought the Truth. It seems too simple, doesn't it?

We're not always willing to simplify our lives. We interpret our angst or fear as evidence that our lives are interesting and full of challenge. Always knowing what's best for us sounds dull, particularly if we have been living on the edge. We can't imagine other people would see us as fun. The excitement of turmoil attracts other interesting people, we think.

Choosing to know what's really best for us is the opportunity made available to us now. Taking it means we will experience everything differently, even though it may look the same on the outside. We won't look dull to others. We will simply look wise.

*If I listen to the Holy Spirit today, I will know
the best move to make.*

Power

 We were created with all power.

We seldom feel the empowerment we've been given. Is that by choice? One would think not; however, we have quite deliberately created the chaotic world we're currently experiencing and in it, we are stripped of real power. This is a confusing concept no doubt. One probably thinks we have power or not, all the time. But we have to remember that we're living an illusion now. Nothing we observe is real or has any meaning. Likewise, the power God created us with doesn't exist in the illusory world.

There is a way to reclaim that power even though we are still here in the illusory world. Seek the guidance of our Creator. When we do that, in fact, we are empowered wholly once again. Does that mean our Creator is here, in this illusory world? His Spirit is, yes. It's that Spirit that resides within us always whom we call the Holy Spirit. With its presence always in tact, we are as powerful as we need to be. When we don't rely on it for our strength, we have none at all. This, too, is true. Which Truth will we be guided by?

I have the freedom to listen to any voice I prefer today.
How each hour develops will reflect
the voice I choose to hear.

Our opportunities to forgive are everywhere.

If we are relying on the ego to interpret the situations that involve us, we'll be consistently misguided into believing we have been attacked. That's the ego's hope, at least, because then we'll be willing to let it determine our response.

Yet, there is another way to perceive the attacks. The *Course* says they are always appeals for healing and help, but what does that really mean? It means the attacker was filled with fear, not arrogance, as we may have supposed. We have the opportunity to envelop that fear with forgiveness.

Depending on the severity of the attack, it may not be easy to turn the other cheek. We may initially refuse, in fact. The resulting chaos doesn't bring us peace though, and we do want peace even when we don't understand how to get it. That's where the presence of the Holy Spirit comes in. It's our avenue to peace in any situation. Every time we forgive another's actions, peace will wash over us.

I will not look hatefully on my attackers today.
I'll see them as needing my help.

February 20

Forgiveness

 To forgive is to know love.

Holding a grudge is so commonplace that we do it unconsciously. We imagine getting even, even for the smallest infractions. Why is this so important to us? There's only one reason. We live, too often, from the ego's perspective rather than the Holy Spirit's, and the ego can't perceive love in its many guises, or the appeal for healing and help. The Holy Spirit performs that miracle for us.

How do we go from holding a grudge to feeling forgiveness? The path is always the same. We can make this simple request: "Holy Spirit, please help me feel and see only love." Making the request as often as necessary is the key to forgiveness. There is no preferred time line. Some days we'll make the journey to peacefulness quickly and efficiently. At other times we'll have to "change our minds" repeatedly.

It doesn't matter how long it takes us to really know forgiveness. Once we do, nothing will ever look quite the same again. Nothing will ever feel quite the same either.

*I will reap the benefit of letting go of grudges
and forgiving others today.*

What we see isn't the Real World.

Because we can touch everything we see, we're baffled to hear it's not real. Time and willingness to suspend our disbelief are necessary to understand this very basic *Course* principle. In fact, we have to accept that we live in a dream, one that quite often feels more like a nightmare. We left the Real World of God behind when we entered this realm.

Now that we're here, so to speak, what's our purpose? This aspect of our existence is simple: We're here to express the love of God. We have no other purpose. It becomes easy when we make the decision, once and for all, to see only love or the cry for it. We'll experience the Real World within our minds when we acknowledge and offer only love.

Peace is as close as our willingness to feel only love. That we'd choose to feel anything else is the ego's work. That we even entered this often insane realm is also the ego's work. Let's ignore the ego! God is always available.

If I see pain or anger or evidence of fear,
I have succumbed to the will of the ego.
Today can be different if I so desire.

In our memory lies the Truth.

No matter what religion we were raised with, we no doubt were told we had never been forsaken by God. *A Course in Miracles*® concurs with that idea; however, it expresses it a bit differently. In its pages we learn that God and all spiritual truths exist within our memory even though we are not conscious of them—unless we specifically seek to remember them. It's comforting to be reminded that God is always present.

Perhaps we're confused about our lack of memory of God. There's an explanation. When the ego split off from the Whole of Creation, it immediately and intentionally forgot from whence it came. But God, being love and only love, didn't forget the ego. It placed in its mind, thus all of our minds, the Holy Spirit as the memory of Him and our real home.

What value does this memory have for us? It's able to remove the sting of the situations we project, providing we tap into it. How? By allowing us a perspective other than the one we've created. God answers our requests every time. We simply have to call.

I'll have the option to remember God in the midst of turmoil today. It will change what I see absolutely.

Happiness

Having a headache and having
cancer are one and the same.

We resist this idea, particularly as it pertains to ourselves or a loved one. But the *Course* tells us "there is no order of difficulty in miracles." All problems are equal and reflect the ego. They exist however we imagine them. Of course, this means they can be as simple or difficult to solve as we decide. "Good fortune" is also the mirror of our mind. Since this is so, isn't it strange that we see so much sorrow and angst?

The good news is that we can use our minds to our advantage just as easily as we use them to our injury. The choice is always open to us. Whatever this day offers can be enjoyed, barely survived, or completely devastating. The perspective we cultivate determines the experience we'll have.

We are much more in the driver's seat than we might have imagined. That might fill us with fear. However, we can eliminate the fear by imagining only love emanating from our companions, our experiences, ourselves. The outer world perfectly reflects our inner picture.

Today I will be as happy as
I make up my mind to be.

Fear or love—there is nothing more.

When we encounter angry family members or mean-spirited co-workers, our instinct is to respond in kind. We forget they are asking for healing and help. Will we ever really change?

Taking just one experience at a time makes change manageable. When someone lashes out at you, first breathe deeply, rather than respond. Next, choose to see your attacker as crying out for love. Then ask the Holy Spirit to show you who this person really is, and respond with love. Following these steps may sound naive or worse, like denial of the situation at hand, but that's because our ego would rather attack whoever is close. Fortunately, the ego isn't the only voice to which we have access.

Categorizing every encounter as either reflecting love or exposing fear clarifies how life works. Accepting responsibility for how we react to others indicates we're getting the message.

I have two options today.
What will I see?
How will I act?

Perception is not a fact.

Thousands of arguments might have been avoided had we known the meaning of *perception*. What we saw seemed real or true, and when others observed the same situation, it seemed sensible to assume that how we saw it was the right way. But now all that's changed, and the impact of this new information has changed our lives forever.

The *Course* informs us that *what* we perceive depends on *who* we put in charge of perception. The ego's watchful eye perceives a darker picture than does the Spirit. When two people are present, both may see through their ego lens. Confusion occurs. Argument results. And the true picture is missed by both.

But what is the true picture? We will always see it when we shed the light of the Holy Spirit on it. The details are never important. The underlying message is always the same: Forgive and feel love and you will feel peaceful.

*I'll perceive peace and joy if I look
through God's eyes today.*

Forgiveness

 Forgiveness merely means changing our minds.

Many of us spend years resenting others' behavior. Maybe a sibling took advantage of us. Perhaps a parent never encouraged us in school. A teacher may have punished us for what a classmate did. A spouse may have had an affair. We can add to this list every day, but what's the point? Does it make us feel better? On the contrary, the more we focus on others' shortcomings, the more prevalent they seem and the worse we feel.

Being in conflict with one person strains our relations with everyone. The absence of peace knows no bounds. More important, what we perceive as being "out there" is really our internal creations.

Whatever happened yesterday or last year or forty years ago can be forgiven and forgotten in an instant. That's the key lesson of *A Course in Miracles*.® We reap what we sow. All that is keeping happiness from us is our resistance to forgiving others. Let's change.

*How I look at my experiences today determines
whether I add any resentments to my list.
I will see only love.*

The body is the ego's projection.

Many of us are critical of our bodies. We perceive ourselves as too tall or too short, too fat or too thin. The list goes on. What we think, however, is what we get: our bodies reflect the message the ego dictates.

This can be confusing. But remember, we tend to focus on our imperfections, and the attention we give them strengthens them. So while we claim to want a better physique or a healthier body, we dwell on how our bodies disappoint us. In the process, we manifest those disappointments.

Stopping a particular thought pattern takes willingness. We need to change our perspective intentionally and radically and stop lecturing ourselves about how we should look. Aligning with the Holy Spirit rather than the ego diminishes the importance of how we look. The miracle is that how we look changes also.

My body is only as real as I make it today.
I am free to think only love.

Imperfections

To see imperfectly is not to see at all.

Our judgment of others comes from not seeing them as they really are. What we see mirrors our own imperfections. If we honored our own perfection, we'd see only perfection in others. What we think we are, we see. What we receive from others, we expect.

Upon awakening, we may look in the mirror and see a body we don't like. Our dismay lingers as we prepare for work. We think about the day ahead and our mind wanders to a contentious co-worker. Unfortunately, these thoughts may make us feel slightly superior; however, we have seen neither the co-worker nor ourselves as we really are.

Do we want to see what's really there? If so, we must ask for the better, true view, first of ourselves, and then of everyone else. If we're mindful about doing this, we'll begin to experience a very different world.

I look but don't really see. I will alter my view today.

Self-acceptance

What we see in others is ourselves.

When we admire men and women, we are often relating to positive qualities that we see in ourselves. However, when we are filled with rage, disgust, or jealousy because of certain traits people have, we don't like the idea that we are seeing "ourselves." Surely, we're not like that!

Only when we join with everyone else, on every level, sharing every trait, do we understand the need for acceptance, our own and everybody else's. Because in our humanness we harbor secret, unlovable characteristics, we are compelled to project them onto others.

The Holy Spirit residing within is God's gift to us, demonstrating God's full and unconditional love. All of our personal qualities, good or bad, are acceptable to God, the Holy Spirit, and Jesus. It's our lesson to learn, and then practice, every opportunity that's available, this same acceptance of ourselves. When we do, we'll begin to feel total acceptance of others too.

Who I see is who I am today.

MARCH

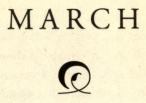

*A full reversal of our thinking
is required by this* Course.

All spiritual paths are governed by a set of principles. This is obviously true of *A Course in Miracles*® also. As beginning students of the *Course,* we may have found some of the principles confusing, even nonsensical. That's perhaps because what we believed in the past is quite dissimilar, in many ways, to what the *Course* proposes. For instance, few if any other paths suggest that this world doesn't really exist. And this principle is key to understanding every other part of this particular path.

It's not easy to give up all past beliefs in an instant. Fortunately, we have all the time we need. Indeed, another *Course* principle is that time doesn't really exist either. Now is all there is. Whenever we come to accept the ideas presented on this pathway, it is absolutely right for us. We'll learn what we need to learn when we really need to know it. But if we are eager to speed our education along, we can request that God assist us. He will. He already has, in fact, by giving us the Holy Spirit as comforter, guide, and Teacher. We're guaranteed that we will understand this path and find our way home when we're ready.

*My old beliefs may still hold me captive, but I can
discard them today with God's help.*

Forgiveness

 Every situation can bring us closer to God.

We have the capacity to bring the Holy Spirit into every situation; all we have to do is request Its presence, love, support. The sting of any circumstance is soothed just as quickly as we turn our attention to God.

Most troubling conditions result from the ego getting out of hand, but the good news is that every problem is an opportunity to turn to the Holy Spirit. The more accustomed we become to relying on the Holy Spirit, the less frequently we'll allow the ego to lead us astray.

There is no time or need for regrets over the ego's transgressions. Forgiveness is why we're here. When we forgive ourselves, as we will when we turn to the Holy Spirit for help, we'll draw closer to the others around us. Seeing our Oneness, loving our sameness, heals all of us.

Getting closer to God is my option today. It's up to me to make the first move.

Ego made the body.

What is our purpose here, in these bodies? Few would dispute that our bodies seldom live up to our dreams of what they should look like. But if our egos "formed" our bodies, why, then, do we perceive our bodies as imperfect?

We're here, in this material realm, to learn. The body is simply our vehicle for learning the lessons we need. It has no other purpose. It has no life of its own.

We are learning, too, that what we see in others, we always project. What part of ourselves projects stunning beauty, which we then hatefully envy, or obesity, which we abhor? Those who have traveled further on this journey than we tell us it's always ourselves, in some form, that we see when we look at others. Let's not forget—we are not separate bodies and separate minds.

In time, we will understand these principles completely. For now, let's simply remember we're here to learn forgiveness. Every situation is an opportunity.

I have the body I've created.
Today I will learn from it.

Problems

 *All problems can be handled
by changing our minds about them.*

For most of us it's a radical opinion, at least initially, to believe that our problems can be relinquished at will. After all, they seem so integral to all the experiences we're having. Indeed they are; however, our experiences mirror our thoughts about ourselves and the people we're with. Problems thus lie with our perceptions.

Being told that we can change our lives by changing our minds seems simplistic. The events that involve us appear far too complicated for such an easy solution. But until we earnestly try to change our minds, we'll not understand the power we garner at the blink of an eye. The Holy Spirit is just as accessible as the ego. If we want to see something, in fact anything, differently, all we need to do is ask the Holy Spirit for a better vision of the circumstance. One will come to us.

Today I choose to change my mind about problems.

Every event is an opportunity for healing and forgiving.

The *Course* tells us that we are here, in this realm, to heal. The people we encounter, the experiences we love and abhor, the dreams that scare or tantalize us—these are not coincidental. We have sought them for the growth we deserve and desire. Along the journey we'll meet "ourselves" repeatedly and every encounter offers us the chance for self-awareness and self-forgiveness.

Some of us will take far longer to heal than others. Our willingness to acknowledge that our reactions to others are mere reflections of ourselves quickens the journey. Our resistance does quite the opposite. How we hate to admit that what bothers us in another reflects our own shortcomings.

Forgiving others mysteriously lessens our own self-condemnation. In time, we realize this is the paramount lesson in our entire journey.

*Today promises me experiences to practice forgiveness.
Each time I do, I'll heal a little bit more.*

March 6

Misbelief

 Shifting our misbelief is our assignment.

Making a *shift* in our thinking is easier to agree to than to do. "Why is that?" we wonder. Perhaps it's because having to *change* a thought implies we were wrong initially. We hate being wrong. Shifting our viewpoint, on the other hand, is quieter and less dramatic, needing little explanation. Fortunately, that's all that's asked of us here.

But what is the misbelief we're courting? In the particular, it's something different for everyone, but in general, all of us are asked to believe that nothing here, in *this* life, really means anything. The experiences are nothing more than simple assignments for learning to believe that the Holy Spirit can answer all questions, smooth all troubled waters, and offer us unending peace. How long it takes us to learn this depends on our willingness to shift our misbelief.

If any situation is causing us stress, it's time to ask for another vision. Until we ask, our belief cannot change.

*A tiny change in how I see something today
can create a big change in my life.*

Spirit is God's creation.

The idea that we decided on the form our bodies would take, that God was responsible only for the Spirit inherent in the form, is awesome and all too elusive. Sometimes we confuse ourselves even more by trying to capture the idea and make it concrete. Not all truths can be concrete. Some simply have to be accepted and, in time, they will be understood.

We can understand now, however, that if God created only spirit, the turmoil we encounter is related to us, not God. That can only mean that it's up to us to disengage from the turmoil. God doesn't do it for us, but if we concentrate on spiritual matters rather than the ordeal of the moment, we will get free of it. Practicing this principle will prove it to us. And this proof will set us free every time we don't like what we are experiencing.

Our lives are simpler when we start to live them from the *Course*'s perspective. Our example can help others to simplify their lives too.

I will look only for the Spirit in the people I meet today.
This way I can avoid all conflict.

Anger

Anger is an unnatural feeling.

Considering how often we may feel anger, it's not easy to understand how it can be judged "unnatural." Most of us would say, "It just seems to happen." That's not the case, however. We create it; it does not have a life of its own. But since it causes us such unpleasant feelings, why would we create it? There's only one answer. The ego, which we also created, wants dominion over our lives. It can control how we think and what we do, when we assent. When it has us angry, it has us in its power.

If we don't want the angst of anger any longer, we do have an alternative. The connection to God can be just as strong as to the ego. We simply have to make the decision to strengthen that tie. We are on the right path currently. We are students of the *Course*. We are spending time with other students and we are meditating upon these ideas. We will get more accustomed to the "natural" feeling of love and Oneness with others as we commit more time to the idea. There is no hurry. Peace and love will keep waiting for us.

I am able to feel love today,
if I seek the Holy Spirit's help.

Joy and peace are natural.

If joy and peace are natural feelings, why do we feel fear and anger so frequently and easily? The culprit is the ego. It likes to keep us in its power; it relishes the separateness it makes us feel. Our vulnerability is always exposed when the ego is in control.

How do we find natural joy and peace? The *Course* says we don't have to look for them. They are present when we are open to the love of the Holy Spirit. There is only one choice we ever need to make, and that's whether to rely on the ego or the Holy Spirit regarding the many details of our lives.

This seems almost too simple. In fact, those among us who have been students for a while say it is simple. Life is only difficult when the ego is leading. Otherwise, it flows smoothly, free of barriers, making us happy and serene every step of the way.

Why would we ever choose to follow the ego when the Holy Spirit is just as close? We'll never have a definitive answer. We don't really need one. Just being aware of our inclination to follow one rather than the other may keep us on the safer course.

*If I'm not joyful today, I have taken the wrong path.
I don't have to stay on it, however.*

Oneness

As we see our Oneness
with God, we heal the world.

If we have always been One with God, why must we see this fact anew, now? Our Oneness is as elusive as this world is illusory. Let's continue to practice attentiveness anyway. Each time we catch a glimpse of our real connection to each other and God, we feel safe, at peace, and complete. This feeling, when expressed to others, fosters peace in them as well. The world is healed by the acknowledgment that we are One.

If seeing our Oneness makes us peaceful, why don't we hang on to this idea? Do we really favor agitation? There is no satisfactory explanation. The ego isn't logical and it's at fault. What we can be sure of is that any feeling we harbor that isn't peace has not been fostered by the Holy Spirit. If our assignment is to heal the world, we'd better figure out how to stay in touch with the Holy Spirit. This isn't all that hard. A simple request for Its presence to be known is all we're asked to do.

℮

My contribution to healing the world rests in my decision
to see the Spirit everywhere today.

Right Mind

Let's be in our Right Mind today.

Is there any other way to be than in one's Right Mind? Before becoming students of this spiritual path, we'd likely have said no. Now we understand that wrong-mindedness has plagued us far too often. What's the evidence of this? We need look no further than the many conflicts we've had with family members or friends. They could never have occurred had we stayed put in the *Right Mind.*

An explanation may be in order. How does one go from the Right Mind to the wrong one? This is nothing more than a shift in our perception. How we see a situation or person indicates which mind we are in. If we see something other than love being expressed, we're not seeing with the Right Mind. It sees only what's true. The wrong mind recognizes all the other expressions and plans our responses accordingly.

Where do we want to be? The mind we settle for is our choice. However, the voice of the ego is strong. Let's remember we'll never be at peace when it interprets our experiences.

It's exciting to recognize we have the option to think however we choose today. Let's have peaceful thoughts.

Holiness

All people are holy.

When we have known abusive men or women, or observed vio-lent attacks between people, it's not easy to accept that all people are holy. Some seem the devil incarnate, in fact. What can it pos-sibly mean that all people are holy? This is one of the *Course*'s teachings that eludes us easily.

It's helpful to remember that what we see, regardless of its intensity, is a form we have created based on the ego's needs. In other words, when we see the "unholiness" in others, we are really only seeing the unholiness we suspect is part of ourselves. The antidote to this depressing vision is forgiveness. Forgiveness that we aren't perfect according to our own assessment, thus forgive-ness of everyone else too. Remember, we are not separate minds and separate bodies; the ego simply makes us think we are.

Deciding to look upon all people as holy today will allow us to see each of them more lovingly, and we'll feel more loving toward ourselves too.

I see only holiness today.
It's my choice.

Peace
Miracles

The ego obstructs miracles.

Why would the ego obstruct a miracle? Because its power lies in mind control. If the mind is willing to be changed, the ego loses control over our feelings, actions, and thoughts. A miracle is nothing more than a changed mind, one that is now willing to follow the guidance of God as expressed through the Holy Spirit. Every time we make a decision, we are choosing either the ego and fear or the Holy Spirit and the miracle of love and forgiveness.

Knowing that our lives can be a series of miracles is exciting. It may also seem unbelievable, particularly if we define a miracle as winning the lottery, or finding the perfect mate, job, or house. When we learn that these outcomes don't necessarily comprise a miracle, at first we're not sure we're even interested. It's then that knowing other students of the *Course* is helpful.

From them we learn that miracles aren't material things but feelings. Experiencing the feeling of love, deep unconditional love, even once creates our desire for it again and again. This miracle can happen as often as we want.

Feeling peaceful today is a miracle I can have regardless of the circumstances in my life.

Judging others

 When we judge others we judge ourselves.

We are trying to learn forgiveness. That's our main lesson, in fact. Our opportunities are numerous because we foist onto others the character defects we abhor and secretly suspect as our own. Then we feel guilty for our projections and await punishment. We may find it hard to believe that God metes out no punishment, but that's what the *Course* teaches.

We punish ourselves enough. Being willing to love ourselves and others is not easy when we first try it. It's good that we have teachers all around us who have already experienced the doubts we have. The teachers are present quite intentionally, we are told. In time, all of this mystery will become clear.

Learning to live free of judgment doesn't happen all at once. Each time we feel "one coming on" we are invited to relinquish the desire to judge. Even those judgments that seem for another's good, aren't—ever! We are always looking at ourselves. No matter what the situation, that's the truth.

Today is the same as all the other days.
I will encounter myself everywhere.
Holy Spirit, help me express love.

Healing our minds is our purpose.

Sometimes we forget just how elementary our assignment on this journey is. It's all about changing our minds. We're actually familiar with changing our minds. We have done it repeatedly throughout our lives. We've changed our minds about friends, neighbors, jobs, spouses. The style of clothes, cars, or houses that appealed to us changed over time. How we've spent our leisure time has changed many times too. So what's the big deal about changing our minds?

This *change of mind* changes everything about our lives. We will see every instance in time differently than ever before. Seeing each person and every event with loving and forgiving eyes allows us to see them as never before. No matter how many times we've looked at a friend or lover, we have not seen that person as we will from now on. Healing our minds is changing them. The miracles will follow.

Asking the Holy Spirit for a change of mind
is my only task today.

March 16

Vengeance

 To harm another is really to harm oneself.

Most of us aren't free yet of the wish for ill to befall others. But we are getting there. Slowly, one experience at a time, we are learning that whatever we wish on others comes to us as well. Our guilt for not being perfect is what triggers our projection. Guilt is such a powerful controller of our actions.

Why do we feel so much guilt? Primarily it's because we allow the ego to do most of our thinking. The ego never wants what's best for us. If it did, it wouldn't hold us hostage, comparing our traits with those of others, judging either us or them as inferior, and plotting our subsequent "success."

We wear ourselves out trying to stay ahead of the pack. How much more exhilarating our lives would be if we moved among our companions blessing them with loving thoughts rather than wishing them harm. We'd immediately feel more peaceful and energized if we expressed only well-wishing.

☉

*I will get further along my path today if I don't
waste time tripping others.*

**Positive thoughts
Right-mindedness**

The gentle heart knows no turmoil.

No one in his or her Right Mind ever experiences anger or frustration. One moment of insanity, triggered by the ego's perspective on the world, initiates all the pain and turmoil we've ever felt. This "wrong-mindedness" is a habit, nothing more. That's good news. We have broken habits many times in our lives. With a bit of effort, we can break this one too.

The quickest way to break a negative habit is to intentionally monitor the thoughts that accompany our behavior. The one controls the other. Keeping our thoughts on a higher plane will keep our behavior up there too. The highest of all thoughts is soft and gentle love. We simply won't create havoc in our lives when we are living them gently. Those we touch with our gentleness will know a new peace too.

*To be free of turmoil is a possibility today. What a gift
I can bestow on those around me.*

March 18

Miracles

Miracles aren't reserved for the few.

The *Course* is perhaps the only source of teaching which lets us know that miracles are available to all of us. What we're learning here is that miracles aren't as mysterious as we'd believed. You don't have to be anyone but who you are to receive one. In fact, you can claim one for yourself at any time you choose.

To receive a miracle takes no more time than an instant. It doesn't take a special prayer, a unique relationship with God, or an extremely unfortunate life. It takes only an open mind and a willing heart.

But what's the process for receiving a miracle? It's asking a simple question. "Holy Spirit, will you please help me see this situation in a more loving way?" *Miraculously,* the new perspective comes. *Miraculously,* the burden of worry or fear or anger dissolves.

A miracle is reserved for me today if I want it.

Perpetual joy is possible.

How can we believe that constant joy is possible? What about a job loss or divorce? The death of a friend or parent? Even getting cut off in traffic or losing a billfold affects our attitude.

The *Course* asks us to do a passionate overhaul of how we think. Fortunately, the overhaul is easier to do than imagined. All that's required is to develop the understanding that "nothing really matters" because *this* experience is merely an illusion. Regardless of how a situation looks, it holds no command over us. The cynical among us will call that denial; however, those who wholeheartedly try it will experience it as joy.

But how can *nothing* matter? Let's remember that we're on a mission in this life. Our experiences are simply learning opportunities. They are meant to teach us, not control how we think or who we are. We are completely in the care of God through the presence of the Holy Spirit in every situation. Joy is our prerogative.

The decision to let whatever happens to be simply noticed,
nothing more, frees me. I am able to do
exactly this today if I so choose.

March 20

Each day is a new beginning.

Being here, now, is all there is. That can be a comforting idea. Whatever disrupted our lives yesterday or when we were children no longer has any control over us. Past experiences are gone forever. If we are haunted by a memory, it's our choice. But why would we want to feel sad or violated or abandoned all over again?

We hang on to the past because we think it defines all that we can be. The *Course* tells us that we are whoever we want to be. It's all in the mind. Being happy and successful and full of love for ourselves and absolutely everybody we meet seems a far-fetched dream. It can be our reality though. How? Simply experience each moment with the help and love of the Holy Spirit. Let *those* eyes see for us. Let *that* heart feel for us. Let *that* voice speak for us.

What makes us mad at any moment is really a past event triggered by the present experience. Why keep living the same old circumstances again?

*I will see today as new. Nothing from my past is
here, now, unless I bring it.*

Knowing the presence of love is the miracle.

When we are feeling love for ourselves, for the people and the experiences in our lives, we are in the midst of a miracle. It is comforting to realize that we can choose to feel love, regardless of our current feelings, if we've made the decision to shift our perception. No experience controls our feelings.

It's easier to feel love, of course, when we remember we are not separate minds and separate bodies in competition for the resources we seek. Knowing and trusting that we are One with the Spirit is very helpful, however infrequently we can do it.

Sometimes we wonder why we ever created the separation. And we're learning that the ego is not really our friend, even though therapists may have said that it needed to be strong. It's good to remember, when we're feeling confused, that we're in these bodies as students. The question to ask is, "What can I learn?"

I am ready for a miracle. Today will be
as peaceful as my mind.

Jesus

We and Jesus are One.

According to old Christian beliefs, to the beliefs still held by many of our acquaintances, the idea that we are the same as Jesus is sacrilegious. How refreshing our new perspective is. It makes Jesus so much more human and accessible, and it allows us to sense our holiness. It also means that the love Jesus felt for all humanity can be transferred to us by a mere acknowledgment of our inner capacity to love.

Knowing that we and Jesus are One also helps us believe we are worthy souls. Jesus, as the teacher, taught love and acceptance. That was his purpose. Forgiveness was also his purpose. Those are our lessons as well. We learn what we will teach; we teach what we need to learn.

In spite of the attacks on Jesus' life, he loved wholly. He saw beyond the attack. He recognized the love of God even when it was invisible to others. We, too, can see only love if that's our choice. Jesus showed us the way. Let's follow his lead.

I am at peace and I will see only love today.

Choice
Conflict

Our level of peacefulness determines our progress.

When we're agitated, we're caught in the ego—we're stuck in old ideas and old behavior. Let's not be too hard on ourselves though. The *Course's* teachings are radically different, in many respects, from what we believed before. Coming to accept these new views is a process. And becoming comfortable using these ideas as tools for more peaceful living takes practice, maybe years of practice. We have all the time we need, however. There is no rush. No one is keeping score.

When someone upsets us, we have a choice: either we can let the ego be engaged and react, or we can acknowledge the other person's need for forgiveness and love, offer it, and go on our way. Our willingness to quietly forgive and love is easier with some people than with others. A gruff boss or a disrespectful neighbor is easy to criticize.

None of us would deny that we'd like more peace in our lives, and it really isn't that hard to attain. Monitoring our feelings and reactions to the events in our lives will reveal our opportunities for greater peacefulness.

I can observe myself in action. Noting what I do or what I think about doing today can teach me to try a softer way.

Generosity
Unconditional love

 To be generous is to be loved.

The *Course* teaches we can only have what we are willing to give to others. We make room in our hearts for more each time we give away what we really want. It's a wonderful principle to live by. It eliminates the fear of scarcity that plagues many of us.

We go through so many stages of want. We begin wanting better toys, then clothes, then friends, then parents. Later we crave better jobs, houses, and spouses. What we have always wanted, however, is unconditional love. We think that if we have all the other things, we'll be guaranteed love too. What we hear now is that we can only be assured of it if we give it away.

Giving away love is a mind-set. It never means giving what we own, or earn, or dream for. It's an attitude we foster. It's an expression we wear on our faces. It's the tone we use when we talk with others. It's who we can be with a little effort.

I will experience only love from others today if I feel
only love in my heart.

Trust

Patience and trust go hand in hand.

We often hear that there are no mistakes, no coincidences, ever. We are told that all events, past, present, and future, serve a purpose. Some experiences eventually fit comfortably into this paradigm. A relationship that abruptly ended or a missed promotion undoubtedly closed doors that needed to close. In time we could see that.

But the experience of physical violence or the devastation of a natural disaster aren't so easily accepted. And when we are worrying about a new job or medical test results, it's hard to be peaceful and patient. At these times we have to help one another remember that we are always getting just what we need when we need it. Perhaps we can't agree that we needed the abuse or the tornado's destruction, but we did learn important lessons from the experience, lessons that we'll likely be called on to share with others.

Remember, we're here to teach and learn. We won't always recognize one from the other.

My trust in the Holy Spirit lets me be patient today.
Nothing will happen for which I'm not prepared.

Judging others

 Let's not judge another.

Every day we catch ourselves in the act of judging someone. The ego loves to make comparisons. It loves to keep us feeling separate, either superior or inferior, competitive, and alone. Otherwise it has no control over what we do and think. Why do we keep giving the ego so much power, particularly when we get nothing good in return? Habits are hard to break, even when they harm us.

God doesn't judge. The Holy Spirit doesn't judge. Jesus didn't judge his enemies. This precedent has been set, and we can follow it too. We have heard many times that humans have only two emotions: love and fear. It's certain that judging others isn't love. And it's fairly obvious why others engender fear in us. Even when we have figured it out, though, what have we learned? We are still left with our feelings unless we make the decision to look with love, as Jesus did, on all the people in our lives. We can do this. It's hard at times but there is a payoff. We'll feel better about ourselves and others right away.

Today I can emulate how Jesus lived. If I slip, momentarily, that's okay. I still have the next minute to try again.

*Nothing is ever missing from our
lives but our awareness of God.*

When the house payment is overdue and our children are truant from school and the job we so desperately wanted went to someone else, it's not easy to believe that all we need is to remember God. The other problems seem so real. And in one respect they are. We do have to acknowledge them and decide on a plan of action. But we don't have to keep our focus on "poor me." Instead, we can recall that the Holy Spirit, God's gift to us, will comfort us and give us guidance.

Whatever is happening around us doesn't have to determine how we feel. We can feel consistently happy and secure, even in the most troubling of times, if we remember we are partners with God, that the Holy Spirit is always present, and that all our experiences serve to teach us. We need not be scared or angry, ever. All is well.

Knowing that God never went away reminds us that when we feel alone, it is only we who have turned away. The solution is simply to turn back.

*Today I will say to God, "Here I am. Tell me what to do."
I'll not be ignored.*

Acceptance

The ego judges.

We all pass judgment on others; that's our human condition. Our opportunity now, however, is to recognize that and to ask to have our perspective changed. The first step is to acknowledge our eagerness to judge. Next comes our willingness to rise above it.

Let's not be ashamed of having an ego. We all have one. Jesus had one too. It's the ease with which we relinquish our ego-driven responses that reveals how much more *divine* than *human* we are.

How we get from being judgmental to being accepting is the journey of our lives. By monitoring what we think and say to ourselves and others, we learn who we are. If we aren't at peace with what we discover, every experience offers a chance to rectify our attitude and our self-perception. It's never too late to take a road less traveled on our journey.

The ego is familiar but seldom my friend.
I'll keep that in mind today.

Perspective

We must discard most of what we have learned.

It's unsettling to discover that we were trained to interpret life's details all wrong. Did our parents, teachers, and religious leaders intentionally steer us wrong? Actually they taught us what they had learned. They meant no harm. Fortunately, we now have a different view. That's all that matters. And it's our assignment to offer our interpretation to others who seek solace and a new direction.

Whatever happened in the past doesn't need to be addressed again. That's a decision we can make. How we felt about our experiences was colored by a perspective we no longer share, so there's nothing to be gained by revisiting them. Forgiveness may be necessary to leave the past behind, and we can do that with the help of the Holy Spirit.

While it's true that some of what we learned may not hurt us, we can't comfortably straddle two conflicting viewpoints. Either we let the ego control our vision, thoughts, and actions, or we let the Holy Spirit. There's no in-between.

My new perspective will make today much more positive.

Defensiveness

 To rise above defensiveness is now possible.

When we are defensive we have let the ego take charge. The ego wants to win, to be right, to control all decisions and people. When the ego encounters other egos, arguments result and we find ourselves getting defensive.

Disagreeing, pouting, resentfully giving in, compromising, and unwillingly negotiating become a way of life for most people. That wouldn't be a problem if it didn't thwart the growth that is the gift of our journey here. Our time here is full of purpose, and we aren't fulfilling it if we are caught in battles of the ego.

Rising above the struggle is as simple as quietly asking for a "second opinion," so to speak, of the situation that's got us agitated. There always is another way of looking at a situation. If we go to the right source, we'll discover it. The only right source is the Holy Spirit.

*Today I can be free of strife. The Holy Spirit will
transform my view of every situation.*

Let's find our Right Mind.

If we're in a power struggle with a neighbor, a boss, a spouse or a friend, we're not in our right mind. It may feel right to be mad. We might feel justified, in fact, but the ego has us in its grip, and that's not our *Right* Mind.

Where is our Right Mind? We probably assumed that our thoughts, whatever their flavor, came from the mind. But that's only partly true. Our mind, according to the teaching of the *Course*, has two parts. In one resides the ego. The Holy Spirit lives in the other. When we are thinking loving thoughts, we're in our Right Mind. When we are thinking anything else, we're not.

We can always find the Right Mind by noting our thoughts, and when we don't like them, we can change them to loving ones. Living in the Right Mind makes our lives so much easier. We have so much more energy for all our work when we are filled with joy rather than anger.

The Right Mind is as close as my wrong mind.
I can change it at will today and be happy.

APRIL

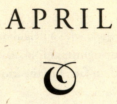

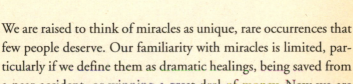

Everyone can make a miracle.

We are raised to think of miracles as unique, rare occurrences that few people deserve. Our familiarity with miracles is limited, particularly if we define them as dramatic healings, being saved from a near accident, or winning a great deal of money. Now we are learning that miracles are available to all of us all the time.

What do we need to make a miracle? Willingness. A change of the mind will result in a miracle every time we are willing to give up the ego's perspective of whatever situation is distressing us. It's very hard to do this at first. We think there's so much at stake. Being right has been important to us. After all, doesn't it define who we are and how worthy we are?

We see that taking the risk of walking away from a situation, rather than "righting it" according to our perspective, is absolutely freeing, once we've experienced it. And that's the miracle.

*I can experience many miracles today if I'm willing
to change my mind.*

April 2

Freedom from turmoil

 We can be in the world but not of it.

Recall how Jesus responded to his enemies while he hung on the cross. We are told he merely observed them and forgave them. He neither felt their attacks nor acknowledged them. His example was to show us the Way. We, too, can look beyond any present experience and see, instead, only the peace of God's world.

We can imagine doing this but seldom do we actually do so. The seduction of anger or worry captures us instead, and we give our lives over to the ego and its nightmare. We need not feel like failures because we do this. We can simply admit to forgetting the better way and try harder the next time we experience a tumultuous circumstance.

Looking at a situation while rising above it gives us immeasurable freedom. Choosing the option to experience only peace changes who we are forever.

*I can be free of all turmoil today. I need not be
affected by anything that happens.*

A healed mind cannot attack.

We are journeying toward healed minds. That's our purpose in this life. Unfortunately, we don't always remember what a healed mind is. That's because maintaining a constant connection to the love of God is elusive and many of us have only brief successes.

Remembering that any person's outburst of anger is a call for healing and help lessens our need to strike back. Of course, the urge to do so may be there, sometimes powerfully so. But with practice we can strengthen our reliance on the Holy Spirit to guide our responses to every person we encounter. We will never want to attack even the most disruptive individuals if we remember the pain that underlies their behavior.

My mind can practice being healed today. I can look with a loving heart on everyone I meet.

Pain

*Any pain we feel comes
from identifying with the ego.*

While it may baffle us, the *Course* says all pain comes from the ego. This is a powerful statement. Can it really be true? What about the injury we sustained while biking or the migraine that followed something we ate? Surely those examples aren't ego controlled. The ego doesn't distinguish between physical or emotional manifestations.

It's helpful to remember what Jesus said about his crucifixion. He saw the wounds but didn't identify with them. With God's help he looked beyond them and forgave those who wounded him. Thus, he felt no pain. The same can be true for us. Where we put our attention is what we will know, feel, and teach.

The level of pain in our lives is our easiest indicator of how ego-aligned we are. The ego is never satisfied. It will always want more money, more friends, more control over others, more success, more attention. That it will go to any length to get what it thinks it deserves is our setup for pain. In some form the pain will come. In some form it will remain until we identify, instead, with the Holy Spirit.

*Nothing will cause me pain today if I look at my life from
the perspective of my guardian Spirit.*

*Our problems come
from wrong-mindedness.*

How can something happening outside of us be due to our own wrong-mindedness? The wreck on the freeway that detains us, the unexpected thunderstorm during our picnic, our grandson's illness while visiting—certainly none of these happenings seem related to our mind. But what the *Course* means is that our minds choose to make problems of situations even though we could choose to see a brighter view.

Our age often indicates how invested we are in our interpretation of life. Seeing it always as happening *to* us rather than just happening indicates our negativity. But can we change? When we reach a certain age, what chance have we got?

It's a good thing we have learned that from the perspective of the *Course*, there is no time, not in the Real World. Everything happens in an instant. What seems like years of thinking one way is merely a flash. We can think something new just as quickly.

*I have no real problems today.
It's my vision that's the problem.*

Healing

A "healer" heals for an instant.

Who are the healers among us? Before our introduction to the *Course*, we likely thought of "healers" as being different from the rest of us, as having extra sensitivity and claiming to understand others better than the others themselves.

It's true that some people are extraordinarily sensitive, but it's also true that all of us are healers. We are learning now that to heal means to love unconditionally and accept being loved; healing happens in the mind. But how does this work?

When friends suffer from physical ailments, we can help them find comfort in the presence of the Holy Spirit. When they are at peace, they will be healed in the best sense of the word. Ailing bodies don't keep us sick. Our attitudes and perspectives do. Each moment is our opportunity for healing, ourselves or someone else. It's all in the mind. In an instant it can change.

I can help a friend heal today by helping him think
a bit differently. How we think is everything.

Jesus laid his body aside.
He didn't die; his body did.

To understand Jesus' purpose and finally our own, we have to first believe that life is changeless, formless, and eternal.

What was the role Jesus played for us? He was the great Teacher who saw not his detractors. This, too, can be our choice. He was Spirit and never felt separate from the Creator. We are Spirit too, inseparable from God. These bodies we carry around, which we'll lay aside one day as Jesus did, are simply our method for communicating with the other bodies we see, other bodies which also are not separate from God or ourselves. It is our opportunity, like it was Jesus' opportunity, to cloak ourselves in peace, to express only forgiveness, to see only love wherever we look.

This may seem impossible to us right now. If we aren't seeking the Holy Spirit's help, it is impossible. But we can reach out now and we'll not be refused. Our Oneness is our purpose. We'll see it.

Today I'll remember that my body is not me;
it's simply my communication tool.

Connectedness

Fear isn't real.

Heart palpitations, clammy hands, a sweaty brow—these are undeniable bodily reactions to an experience. However, our misinterpretation of the circumstance triggered the reactions. Nothing fearful was actually happening.

As initiates to the *Course,* we may not rest easy with this information. What we're barely beginning to grasp is that the outer world is always the product of our inner dialogue. In due time we'll gladly claim responsibility for everything we experience. Finally, then, fear will no longer haunt us.

In the meantime, it will help if we focus on our connectedness to everyone we encounter. When we see other people as nothing more than reflections of ourselves, we'll agree that we have nothing to fear from them. They aren't separate bodies out to harm us or make us afraid. Seeing us as one eliminates our discomfort.

*If I feel afraid today, I will pay heed to
how I see others.*

All problems are solved when
brought to the light of the Holy Spirit.

We bring the easiest of our problems to God with little resistance. A minor argument or a traffic jam doesn't hinder us for long because we accept them as being beyond our control. Letting them go isn't difficult.

We'd get exactly the same result if only we'd apply the same principle to bigger problems. The situation would change, our anxiety would dissipate, and we'd know peace. Bringing any experience to the light of love teaches us that we are safe, that it is meant for our good, and that we needed it to complete our journey.

When a loved one leaves us or our boss unexpectedly dismisses us, it's hard to keep faith. It's even harder to keep the ego from trying to change the decisions. The *Course* tells us that our "changed mind" is a process, often a slow one. Bringing our easier problems to the Holy Spirit is a good beginning. We will change.

I can get some good practice at bringing my problems to God today.
The problems will change.
So will I.

Physical world

Our bodies are not who we are.

We live in a culture that extols the body. Television, magazines, and advertising of all kinds preach the importance of the body and the necessity for it to be curvaceously slim and seductively attractive. It's not easy to dismiss all of these messages.

The paradox is the less we focus on our bodies, the more they seem to satisfy us. How does this work? The main idea of the *Course* is that the only thing that's real is Spirit. Our bodies are nothing more than the ego's invention to get us around in this material world, which also isn't real. And because our bodies are an extension of the ego, we're hindered by all the fear-induced data that the ego manufactures to control the circumstances of its environment.

When we have a contusion on our leg or a rash over our midsection, it's hard to agree that our bodies aren't real. We see an image in the mirror, and we respond to being pinched. Let's try to suspend our disbelief on this matter. Acknowledging only Spirit will get easier. And better, it will reward us many times over.

My body is my learning module. It is not me. My Spirit wears my real identity today.

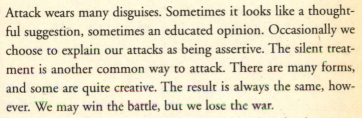

Attack or love, that's all there is.

Attack wears many disguises. Sometimes it looks like a thoughtful suggestion, sometimes an educated opinion. Occasionally we choose to explain our attacks as being assertive. The silent treatment is another common way to attack. There are many forms, and some are quite creative. The result is always the same, however. We may win the battle, but we lose the war.

Choosing love, the alternate response, isn't so hard once we make up our minds to try it. It becomes even easier to choose it again once we've made the initial selection. And it is much less stressful. It doesn't take an elaborate plan to approach the other person or circumstance. We simply put our heart first and the rest follows.

I have an easy day ahead if I give only love.

Faith

We are told all we need to know.

We often crave to know every detail of every moment of the rest of our lives, but we don't need them. We couldn't handle them, really. We are given all the information we need as the moments tick by. The Holy Spirit knows far better than we what we need to know, and when. And we'll always find it out when the time is right.

When we grow in our acceptance of this principle, our lives will grow simpler. Our task is to turn to the Holy Spirit, not the ego, for direction. Our minds contain them both, of course. Recognizing their separate voices comes with practice and the willingness to be peaceful rather than "right."

Our lives don't become less exciting when we let the Holy Spirit be in charge. In fact, some might say that going along for the ride, rather than steering the car, offers us unexpected adventure and surprise.

Letting someone else decide the route leaves me free to enjoy the many stops on the way.

*If we are afraid, we have
dropped the hand of Jesus.*

Virtually every day we have a moment or two of confusion, or worse. Perhaps a friend or colleague suddenly erupts in anger and scares us. Will we be blamed for someone else's unhappiness? The burden of keeping everybody happy weighs heavily on us. It need not be like this, however.

With perseverance, we can learn to recognize when we are ill at ease. In those moments of dread we can *take the hand of Jesus* and move forward. All we must do, in essence, is remember that we are not alone; we have to do nothing alone. The quiet help of the ever-present Inner Voice can ease our minds and direct our decisions.

Not having to be afraid, ever again, seems almost too good to be true, doesn't it? But that's the promise the *Course* makes to us. All we have to do is our part. We begin by opening our hands and minds.

*I do want to be at peace today. If I'm not,
I'll remember why and remedy it!*

Guidance

 It's never too late to change our minds.

Guilt over mistakes and missed opportunities plague most of us. For some reason we expect to conquer every challenge, to know unquestionably how to solve every problem the first time we encounter it. We can fully understand that children need to practice walking and catching a ball and eating with a fork before they can master these skills. But we're adults. We think we must get it right the first time.

It's so comforting to learn that we can change our minds midstream, and try a new tack with no blame. Asking for help from the Holy Spirit, following what we think the guidance is, and then discovering that we're not really happy doesn't mean we have made an irreparable error. We can ask for help again and start over.

We are too hard on ourselves. If only we could love ourselves as much as the Holy Spirit does, we'd be gentle and accepting of our human traits. We're doing the best we can. Our willingness to stay in touch with the Spirit is what improves our performance.

I have the freedom to switch courses whenever I want.
If I'm not sure of the direction to take,
I'll ask for guidance today.

Giving is not quantitative.

Being giving is an attitude. Some people give more willingly than others. When we extend our generosity only to those persons we love, we're really not being giving at all. What we withhold from one, we withhold from all.

Does this mean we have to be giving even toward those who hurt us? Ultimately, yes. Just as Jesus looked beyond his wounds while on the cross, we must look beyond our hurts as well. Perhaps we can't do this right now. And that's okay. Praying for the willingness to forgive is enough for the moment.

What we realize after a time is that we can develop a giving spirit. Thinking only love and forgiveness creates more love and forgiveness. It's very freeing too: we don't have to decide how to behave, what to say, how to feel if we have first made the decision to love and forgive. What we get in return are good feelings about ourselves and acceptance from others. But even if it's not forthcoming, we will not even notice in time.

*I will give love and acceptance to everyone today,
even when I don't really want to.*

April 16

Purpose

If we believe we have a purpose,
we can dispel our fear.

The first stage of believing may be the decision to do so. We may need to make that decision every day, even many times a day. We do have a purpose. That's why we're all here. And those of us who travel this path are on a very special mission, in fact. It is our job to forgive and love, and through our example, others will be attracted to do the same thing.

Our lives can be far less complicated than we make them. We get caught in believing that life's tiny details matter when they don't. Even a rageful battle with an ex-spouse or a power struggle with a child doesn't really matter—except to the ego! The ego always wants to win. The ego is always ready to wage war. And our fear about not being in control keeps us listening to the ego.

How refreshing to give up the battle once in a while. Some circumstances will be easier to pass over than others, that's true. But doing it even once is a beginning. That's all we need.

I may not know the details of my purpose today
so I'll keep it simple. I'll offer only love.

*A miracle is merely a shift,
a change, in perception.*

How hard can it be to "change our minds"? Our personal histories would suggest that we have changed our minds many times. We've moved, changed jobs, changed marriages and relationships, left friends behind. But the *Course* says we're ready for a new understanding of what "change" means.

Life changes were generally the result of an active ego. Some of the changes may have been positive. However, if the ego inspired them, they weren't miracles. They were still attempts to control our lives or the lives of others. Real miracles come from changing our minds, not other people or situations. We are learning the difference now.

The shift in perception we are learning about engages only our hearts, never the ego. We need merely to ask for the shift and it will come; our request is granted. The Holy Spirit wants us to be peaceful, to have the miracle. Let us ask for it.

I can have one or more miracles today.

Mistakes

God is the ultimate Teacher.

The *Course* manual says that we are God's Teachers. Perhaps we feel deficient in this role because of the mayhem still evident in our lives. Let's not forget two things: People typically learn their most crucial lessons from watching others make errors, and mistakes are instructive if they are acknowledged.

We believe that God is the ultimate Teacher, but how do we actually learn from Him? It's far easier than we might have imagined. When we watch friends or strangers behave caringly, not selfishly, toward others, we are seeing God in action. We can follow their lead. When we are faced with a situation that demands a decision or a response, we can quietly ask God to lend us a hand. We'll intuitively feel the best answer from within.

The Holy Spirit, which rests in our minds, is God's special tutor for our education here. We are never out of Its range when there's learning to be done.

I will be attentive and loving to others today.
That is God's key lesson for me
and everyone else.

Prayer is often arrogant.

When we're being honest we'd probably admit to praying for highly specific outcomes in our relationships, definitive solutions to a nagging health problem, or a longed-for career promotion. When we haven't detailed our desires, we worry that God won't answer us to our specifications. We are certain that we best understand what we need.

The *Course* never says that how we pray is wrong, rather, that it is folly and surely arrogant of us to second-guess the Ultimate Authority. The ego is the voice that dictates conditional prayers, but as we become more willing to listen for the Holy Spirit's guidance, we'll understand that the only thing we ever need to pray for is peace.

We will accept and eventually understand whatever is occurring in our lives if we seek and relish the peace that we're certain to receive if we pray for it. We are *here* as students. Let's enjoy the simpler path to understanding.

I will seek only peace today.
No matter what experience troubles me,
peacefulness will see me through.

Giving

What we give, we get.

We have all experienced rejection or betrayal after offering love and support to a friend or co-worker. That's because human behavior is often flawed. Our positive actions don't always return to us like a boomerang. Why, then, does the *Course* say that we get what we give? The one we love may not offer love in return right now, but we will feel loved and accepted by others in our lives.

What we may get shouldn't determine what we give today. Let's remember that we are not really separate minds and separate bodies, thus what we give or withhold from someone today we are really doing to ourselves. There are even instances when we may think we deserve punishment, but punishing ourselves punishes everyone. This concept is elusive but helpful because it simplifies our choices when we are deciding what to say and do.

What we give, what we project, comes back to us, sometime, somewhere. We can determine the kind of life we are going to have.

I have much more control over what comes to me than I may have thought. Today will give me many opportunities to see this.

The Holy Spirit is always present.
It is we who close the door.

Why would we ever close the door on the Holy Spirit? In our more conscious moments, we wouldn't, of course. However, we drift into unconsciousness without even realizing it. And that makes us easy prey for the ego, the indomitable door-closer.

The ego wants to be in charge of our lives. The strength of its pull is evidenced in the many battles we have with other people on the job, in the neighborhood, or at home. We grow too accustomed to lives of strife, experiencing fear daily or hourly. Many people we journey with likewise struggle. We consider it normal.

Fortunately, we each know people who are more peaceful than we. Close observation generally reveals they don't engage in conflict. They move away and smile. The Holy Spirit has spoken and they have listened.

Listening to the Holy Spirit is always an option.
Why not today?

April 22

Problems

 We know neither the problems nor the answers.

In this human form, which is dictated by the ego, we are distant from the Real World that governs our lives. On this particular journey, however, we are on an educational path to all knowledge, to ultimate Reality. Misunderstanding the circumstances of this daily existence is to be expected. How fortuitous that the Holy Spirit has been placed in our minds to guide our journey.

It's the human condition to assume we can not only understand our problems but also define the solutions. Being told in the text of the *Course* that we can do neither offers us relief. Not knowing the problems or the answers doesn't mean that we're in a hopeless condition. On the contrary, it means we don't have to figure out our lives. It will be done for us, safely and peacefully, if we listen with our hearts.

Today will be far more peaceful than my ego would make it if I listen with my heart to the soft voice within.

Everything that happens today is helpful.

Perhaps we can accept that the loss of a job which was highly stressful or the death of a parent who was gravely ill can be helpful, at least from a philosophical standpoint. But how can every occurrence be helpful? If we have an automobile accident or a fight with a friend, it doesn't feel helpful.

We are learning, slowly, that our lessons, which are contained in the circumstances of our lives, are never meant to hurt us, just educate us. We adjust to this knowledge with the help of others who seem far more peaceful than we. Probably they have already learned that there are no accidents.

Our first reaction to any unexpected encounter is often resistance and fear. That's okay. That doesn't mean we can't change. The more we trust that everything is helpful, the less afraid we'll become.

Everything I experience today will benefit me.

Forgiveness

How open-minded are we?

Being open-minded generally means we're tolerant of people who hold political opinions and spiritual beliefs other than our own. Open-mindedness also includes accepting that both genders and all races are inherently equal. But the *Course* says there's more to it.

The *Course* defines open-mindedness as total forgiveness of everyone for whatever their transgressions. That's not so easy. The reason we struggle with this principle is that we severely judge ourselves. Our imperfections aren't tolerable to us, so no one else's are either. As we accept what we hate about ourselves, which we project onto others, we'll become more willing to offer compassion, first to others and, finally, to ourselves.

Today I will practice forgiveness.
That's the Course's *main lesson.*

One with God

We live in God.

What does it mean to say we live *in God?* We wonder about the havoc in our lives. It can't be part of God. The worry and anger we feel can't be either. From where does the turmoil arise?

Our real home is with God. We never actually left it; however, according to the *Course* teachings, the mind took leave from God in a single moment and created this world we're inhabiting. There's no adequate explanation as to why. It just happened. And now we long for the changeless, eternal home of God; fortunately, our experiences with one another are the pathway back, providing we seek our direction from the Holy Spirit.

We don't have to struggle with our companions. We don't have to worry about tomorrow. We don't have to notice disharmony. Even now we can be at home with God if we settle for peace rather than winning an argument. That's the good news.

If I believe I am with God now,
I'll behave accordingly.
Today can be quite a treat.

April 26

New insights

 Unlearning lessons of the past is our challenge.

Whenever we learn something new, it changes ever so slightly how we view everything in our lives. Nothing that we hold dear and true is unaffected by the incorporation of a new idea. We are overwhelmed at first with the new information we encounter with the *Course*. Must we toss out everything and start over?

If we could, perhaps that would be easiest. However, we don't have to. We simply need to acknowledge that the ego did most of our interpreting in the past and it didn't serve our spiritual interests. The ego strengthened selfishness. We focused our attention on scarcity and blame, thus fear predominated. Our actions didn't nurture our companions or ourselves. We learned so much that was "wrong." Can we really unlearn it?

I will embrace the Course *one idea at a time. Today everything that happens is for my good.*

Forgiveness is the path to peacefulness.

Coming to believe that all disharmony may be the result of even a single, still-harbored resentment gives us a refreshing new look at our lives. We are only as upset as our willingness to let old memories control us. We can be free of them—now! It's a decision to let the past go. It's a decision to ask the Holy Spirit for a new perspective. It's a decision to ask, again and again, if we fall into the old, more familiar pattern of disharmony.

Who among us would admit to preferring agitation to peacefulness? Few at best. However, many of us live as though that's the case. We get mad and stay mad. We argue and then relive the tension for hours or days. New experiences with unsuspecting companions carry the stamp of earlier encounters that left us furious. We can change all of this. It's not so very difficult, in fact.

The Holy Spirit is always with us. Of course, so is the ego. Which one we honor will determine our level of peacefulness.

I will be as peaceful as I decide today. Getting free of resentment through forgiveness is the key.

Fear triggers attack.

Any attack, whether verbal or physical, is caused by fear. When contemplating an attack, we need to ask ourselves, "What is causing the fear?" That's the issue to consider, and the answer is always the same. Fear occurs when we align ourselves with the ego. Fear has no life of its own.

The urge to attack another person is manageable. We can always curtail the impulse if we are willing to seek the help of the Holy Spirit. Its voice is softer than the voice of the ego, so we have to grow quiet to hear it. But we'll see our "opponent" quite differently after listening to the Spirit.

The Holy Spirit is capable only of love. If we are not at peace in a situation, or if we harbor any thought other than love, we are not aligned with the quiet voice. The only barrier to feeling love is the one the ego constructs. We are lucky that its voice can be ignored in an instant.

The voice I hear today determines my level of peace.

Our belief in separateness creates our problems.

Why do we resist our Oneness with all humanity? For one thing, it's hard to conceptualize. We can certainly see separate bodies. Our differences of opinion suggest different minds. Our divergent hopes for the future and memories of the past imply different personalities. And yet, we are told, we are One. How can this be?

Another disturbing suggestion is that the qualities we abhor in others, we share in some aspect. This idea probably pleases none of us. But if we accepted it more willingly, perhaps we would not judge others so harshly. That might be the first step in drawing closer to them, which in turn might be the first step in acknowledging how alike we are, in other words, the Oneness we share.

Often these feel like esoteric ideas. We can't expect to understand this new vision of how life really works in a single instant. But suspending the ego's judgment, as often as necessary, will in time move us closer to a new, far more peaceful vision. Suddenly it will seem as though we have understood it all along.

*Acknowledging my connection, my sameness, my Oneness
with another person will comfort me today.*

Guilt

We reinforce our guilt when
we project it on to others.

Where does guilt come from? We are told it comes from our separation from God and thus one another. We instinctively sense that the separation is wrong; guilt is our payback. The idea of this separation is hard to understand at times. If we didn't want it, why did we create the illusion? The ego has the answer. The ego wanted control of our lives. And it reigns supreme until we choose to ignore its urges.

When we're in the company of the Holy Spirit, which is our prerogative at any instance, we feel no guilt. We feel no anger or hurt or fear either. When we're *with* the Holy Spirit, we feel only love and we forgive all attacks, our own or others.

Why do we wander away from the Holy Spirit? When we feel so serene and secure there, why would we leave? That's the insanity of our humanness. We think we deserve more and the ego tricks us into believing that's so. The sad truth is that we end up with less. Our good connections to others are soon gone because of the jealousy the ego inspires.

The only sensible thing to project on another is love.
Every person I meet today is my opportunity.

MAY

*Miracles are shifts in
the mind's perception.*

We have all heard a story of someone who was cured of cancer. Wouldn't that be a miracle in the body? Some might argue yes; however, many would say a change in the body has to be precipitated by a change in the mind. If illness is all one thinks is possible, illness is what one gets. Thinking health and well-being might not make a disease disappear, but the person's healed mind and attitude will guarantee a peaceful response to life.

Learning that miracles happen in our minds should bring comfort to all students of the *Course*. It means we are all privy to them, whenever we want, regardless of the circumstances hindering us.

*I'll monitor my mind's work today.
What I think is all-powerful.*

Caring for others

 Joining with others is how healing occurs.

To take another's pain away is not our assignment. That doesn't mean we should turn our backs on those who suffer or judge them negatively for their struggles. The best response, the only loving response, is to follow the guidance of the Holy Spirit in regard to the dilemmas of others: be a loving presence in their lives. *Be with them where they are, nowhere else.*

Joining with others in this way acknowledges our Oneness. When we see and celebrate this togetherness, we reduce the strife in everyone's life. The *Course* tells us that none of us go home until we all go home. Bonding with all others speeds the journey home. But what does "going home" mean? It means being at peace, total peace, in the Real World.

Grasping the difference between the Real World and the one the ego inhabits is the door to a hope-filled, serene life. A mere nod in the direction of this door swings it open. The view is fantastic. So is our memory of it.

*As one heals, we all heal. I will extend my hand
to a sister or brother today.*

All but Heaven will fall away.

Our destination is Heaven. We may not acknowledge this. We may not realize it, in fact, because most of us are stumbling through our experiences just trying to hang on. Understanding that we all are journeying to One Home eases the fear and subsequent pain we feel on occasion. We are learning that our lives make sense, and that we are sharing this trip with our Teachers. We are not traveling alone.

Real solace comes in discovering our connectedness to others. Unfortunately, it may take a long time to appreciate this. The isolation we cultivate, often out of fear, obstructs our vision of the Real World. We are learning that the experiences we walk through serve only as steps to Heaven, and the steps yet to be climbed are as few or as many as our resistance to them demands.

Every day brings us closer to the peace of Heaven. Let's be grateful for that push to reach for each other or for the hand of God. It's always extended.

What does Heaven look like? I'll get a glimpse today if
I seek the comfort of God's extended hand.

Others' faults

Others' faults inform us of who we are.

We resist the idea that the traits we abhor in others are our own. They simply can't be! But the wiser ones on this journey say, "Think again." The fault in our thinking comes from believing in separation. As long as we see other people as having separate bodies and separate minds, we will not understand that who we see is a reflection of some aspect of ourselves.

Being convinced, finally, that we are One comes from our willingness to suspend our disbelief. Accepting this as truth comes more easily with even a little effort.

Faults exist only in the ego. They have no life outside of that. They are illusory, absolutely. But they seem so real, we think. How cunning is the ego. Fortunately its strength doesn't match the strength of the Holy Spirit, whose perception wipes out all illusion. Going to It for help is the only requirement for eliminating faults, ours and those we imagine others to have.

I must remember that I am who I see today and every day.

Be still and know.

What does it mean to be still? What are we trying to know? These are serious questions. Having minds that run nonstop seems the norm. It's who we are, after all. Experiencing the quiet within feels like doing nothing. And we've been programmed to think we need to be doing something all the time. To stand still is to get left behind, we think.

Let's pretend for a spell that it's okay to be idle. Let's take this as an opportunity for a new way of living. With every thought that comes, let it float away. With every desire to speak, let the moment pass. Every movement can be forfeited. Feel the freedom of doing nothing, saying nothing, thinking nothing, for even a few moments. Peace does come. Peace at last.

We can't be sure we'll know anything specific in this quiet, but we will know what we need to. Within the quiet lie all answers.

I will give up my mad thinking
for a few moments today.

Anger

 To forgive is to join with others.

No doubt at least one circumstance will arise today that can trigger anger. Even minor disturbances push our buttons if we're not vigilant. The question many of us have is, "What's wrong with anger?" We've heard that it's healthy to admit anger, that we shouldn't stuff it. Have we been misguided?

From the *Course* we learn that anger is about us, not the others on our path. Therefore, expressing it by attacking someone else doesn't properly address the cause. If we're the sole source of what is irritating us, we're also the single source of forgiveness, and thus change and healing. Actually, this simplifies our lives. It just isn't possible to make others behave, but it is possible to change how we act, feel, and think. The unexpected miracle is that everything and everyone else will be changed in the process.

I am as happy as I choose to be today. My anger is gone when I acknowledge its source and its solution.

Our pain has value.

We find it difficult to accept that pain can have value. Surely we don't want the migraine headache, the mysterious illness, the broken heart. Our wise teachers suggest that the ego creates and hangs on to pain to get its needs met.

We're learning now that our unmet needs are really our unneeded desires. What we think we need and what we actually need are seldom the same.

The *Course* says all we need is love. Our attempts to get love from relationships or through possessions fail, so we seek sympathy and attention for our pain and call this love. The ego stops at nothing to get what it wants, even sacrificing our health.

Our pain will leave us when we focus on forgiveness and giving only love to others. Removing the focus from ourselves miraculously cures us by healing how we think. This will do for us what no amount of ego effort can do.

I can decide I don't need whatever ails me today.
The ego does me no favors.

Attaining the Real World is a long process.

The Real World isn't a place even though we speak of it as though it were. It's a state of mind, a peace-filled, loving state of mind. We shouldn't be surprised that it eludes us. We have had extensive experience inhabiting the more conflicted, anxious state of mind. Our discomfort there has often been great but always familiar. It's hard to leave the familiar.

Part of our difficulty as newcomers to the *Course* is in understanding how we can get from one state of mind to the other. Many of us are accustomed to thinking we can't change. Many of our acquaintances are as stuck as we are. Often, we assume that something monumental must occur for us to see our lives differently. Indeed, that might help, but fortunately, it's not necessary.

Moving from one state of mind to the other happens in a flash, but we seldom reside in the Real World long. The ego has such a strong hold on us. Wanting peace has to be more attractive to us than wanting power. Some days it is.

I can experience a peace-filled world today.

One choice is all we ever need to make.

Because we feel bombarded by the changing circumstances of our lives, we tend to see them as far more complicated than they really are. Out of habit we try to make perfect decisions about many situations instantly. Our frustration and accompanying anxiety convinces us that every detail of life is critically serious. Of course, it isn't.

On the other hand, our daily experiences are important. Our experiences hold great purpose. We will discover what we need to know, and we will teach that which we have already learned if our hearts are open to the messages of the Spirit.

Our lives will be filled with joy and insight if we approach them with wonder, hope, and acceptance. The choice to see all experiences accordingly is the only choice that makes sense.

಄

The choice to simplify or complicate my life is solely mine.
Today will evolve as chosen.

Attitude

This world is the product of our minds.

We have often heard, "You get what you expect," "As you think, so you are," "Attitude is everything." Hearing this message one more time is reassuring.

But what if the world we see is scary and threatening harm? It's not easy taking responsibility for these results. There is a way to change what we see, however, regardless of the dreadful details. We can seek the help of our minds. We know that the mind is both ego and Holy Spirit, not necessarily in equal portions. If our outlook is brooding and bleak, the ego is inflated. If our outlook is hopeful and loving, we sense the Holy Spirit's presence in our lives. We also need to remember if we feel physically threatened the most loving thing we can do for ourselves is to protect ourselves by moving away from a dangerous situation.

We can move from one side of the mind to the other at will. This makes our world our choice.

I will do my part to heal the world today.

The Holy Spirit always speaks to us.

When we're in the midst of an argument or panic attack, we may be slow to remember an immediate solution: quieting our minds to hear the guidance of the Holy Spirit. It will always offer us the calmness we need. Unfortunately, Its voice is seldom as loud as the ego's. That's why it takes willingness and commitment to change how we listen if, indeed, we are to experience the serenity we deserve.

Just knowing the Holy Spirit is always there is the first lesson in our new way of living. Practicing a method of meditation or relaxation can help us quiet our minds so we can listen for guidance. When the really hard stuff comes along, like the loss of a job or the dissolution of a friendship, we'll be able to collect our thoughts and know the feeling of peace in a tiny instant. All we'll have to do is stop, breathe deeply, and listen.

Today I will listen for the Holy Spirit's guidance.

Relationships signify our spiritual health.

We are in relationships with many people. Each relationship foretells the degree of our connection to God. We may feel more comfortable in one relationship than another; however, if we are not peaceful in one of them, we are not truly peaceful in any, even those that seem fun and easy.

But just as the weakness of one relationship signifies the weakness of all of them, wholly mending just one also heals them all, in an instant. The *Course* teaches that there is only one relationship. This relationship has simply taken many forms.

Looking beyond the characteristics of a single relationship to the spirit that abides within it allows us to join with everyone in love and gratitude. We will not feel tense. We will not entertain conflict when we appreciate the inner holiness of us all.

I only have to mend one relationship today for all of them to be healed. Surely that's possible.

*To heal is to recognize
our unity with all others.*

What we have yet to understand and embrace is our connection to each other. Because we continue to see individual bodies, we continue to experience individual comparisons. It's this perception of separateness, of the subsequent inferiority or superiority one feels, that "sickens" the mind. The *Course* offers a single prescription for any ailment: *See only love and Oneness in God.* It's really that easy.

How do we change the way we look at others? It's best to begin with ourselves. Appreciating our own Oneness with God gets us started. Once we feel that connection, we can imagine connecting with others too. Then we must practice. With as much compulsion as we used to devote to judging others, we must now love others as ourselves.

*I can help to heal the world by how I
see my brothers and sisters today.*

Purpose
Healing the world

 Our purpose is simple.

Complicating our lives is so typical. We feel driven to analyze every feeling we or others have. We search for the hidden meaning in a co-worker's comments. We fearfully assume that our "job" in this life is enormous and we probably can't succeed. We think that others lie in wait for our mistakes in order to judge us. The list goes on. Yet how wrong our perceptions are!

We don't have a grand assignment, and others aren't watching us. The only task is a small one, and it's the same for all of us: to speak, think, and act lovingly at every moment. We need not write the definitive book or discover a cure for cancer. We aren't expected to solve a neighborhood's crime problem or settle a three-generation feud. Giving and receiving only love fills the bill.

If all the people we meet actually fulfill this assignment, and everyone they meet does likewise, the experience of the entire human race would be quite different. The change can begin with only one. Let it begin here, now, with me.

I can make a difference today in my response to
the people I meet. Peace can begin with me.

Every problem is due to unforgiveness.

Automobile accidents, overdue bills, unemployment, skin cancer—how can all these problems be attributed to unforgiveness? Those who are wiser than we, however, proclaim that unforgiveness is the root of every problem.

Perhaps we don't have to understand the subtlety of the statement right now. Certainly, the ego won't concur with it, but the ego has led us astray myriad times before. That's its job. Let's accept, for today at least, that we need to work on forgiveness throughout our relationships. This includes our current ones along with those that have long since passed. Forgiveness can only make our lives less stressful.

We have all experienced the relief that comes from mending the fence with a co-worker or spouse. Let that awareness convince us that all relationships, all experiences in fact, would feel softer, more loving, if we were in a state of love and gratitude and forgiveness.

Today it's time to practice forgiveness.
Every tomorrow will profit from it.

Guidance

 Do nothing without the counsel of God.

When we take stock of our past, we recoil from many of the memories. In some instances, we felt victimized. In others, we were the perpetrators. Whoever was the culprit in each situation failed to seek the counsel of God. Had the voice of the Holy Spirit been sought, a hurtful act would never have been committed.

It's possible that we can act in a loving manner even when we fail to seek proper guidance. We can't be certain, however, that we are doing so. Thus, the safest avenue is to ask for the Holy Spirit's wisdom and then wait. It will always come, but not necessarily as quickly as we think we need it. That's what often triggers the ego to get into the act. Its impatience moves us to force control, and unfortunate outcomes result.

God promises that we'll move through our experiences safely and that we'll learn what we need from them if we choose Him as our companion. Life can be satisfying when we journey in good company.

I won't be faced with struggle or confusion today
if I seek proper counsel.

Our minds create the visible world.

Whatever we see, we cause. If we aren't happy with our experiences, we need to put our minds to work again and re-create a world that gives us more pleasure.

What we have to guard against when we change our lives is not letting the ego have center stage in our minds. The ego will never foster harmonious circumstances unless it can selfishly benefit from them. Our minds respond to two voices. The conflicts and troubling situations have their roots in the ego. The peaceful periods come when we willingly, or perhaps unwittingly, pay homage to the Holy Spirit.

Even the least reflective of us can see the payoff offered by each voice. It may be that we want turmoil occasionally; that's always our option. The more time we take to reach the peace we deserve, however, the slower the process for everyone else too. Let's not forget: *No one goes home until we all go home.*

I am in charge of my life today. How I choose to live will affect everyone else I meet.

Perspective

What you see is what you want to see.

Those men and women who are always singing the blessings of life are not luckier than we are. We may think they are if we are feeling sorry for ourselves, particularly if they just got a raise at work and we got laid off. But the only real difference between them and us is vision, and that doesn't mean eyesight.

We create our world. Every situation we confront is what we've "asked" for. Those we befriend, and even those we dread, are people we unconsciously need to know. What we experience, moment by moment, reflects the inner world of dreams or fears that consume our minds. Our lives are personally engraved. Since that's how it works, why aren't we always singing our blessings too? Why have we chosen these painful situations?

We may find no satisfactory answer for how our lives have unfolded up to now. They are what they are, and we are responsible, but today is a new day. Tomorrow is too. There is time to create a new vision.

I will see only love if that's my choice.
Today has only just begun.

Being aware of love's presence is our lesson.

Many situations in life seem unloving. A hateful reply to a question, for instance, never feels loving; nor does a reprimand. Subtle slights from friends, like unreturned phone calls or frowns instead of smiles, belie their claims of love. With so many examples of seeming lovelessness, how can we grow more aware of love's presence?

The *Course* tells us that every expression one makes in life is either love or a cry for healing and help. Learning to identify love is perhaps easier when we are able to recognize its opposite. Just knowing that every action is one or the other clarifies our understanding.

If what we experience from another person doesn't feel like love, it probably isn't. What it is, however, is an opportunity, always, for us to offer love in the form of forgiveness anyway. It's not difficult to do so, except at first. The rewards we'll reap will strengthen our desire to make the decision on a regular basis. Best of all, we'll be showered with more love from others.

Looking for signs of love or appeals for healing and help
will inform all my experiences today.

Ego

To give is to receive in kind.

Blasting the horn at a slow driver or yelling at a neighbor girl for running through our flowers may give us short-term satisfaction. We may feel righteous at the time, but when the moment has passed, we're generally a little ashamed. Why do we allow the ego so much power over our actions?

When we respond negatively to any experience, we have let the ego take charge. It loves to keep us agitated because then we stir up trouble. Our inner peace quickly disappears and we're completely at the mercy of the ego.

It helps some of us to think of the ego as an enemy. The contrast between the ego and the loving comfort the Holy Spirit offers is profound. The difference we would feel throughout our day-to-day experiences is, likewise, profound.

I am in charge of my thinking and my emotions. The choice to follow the ego or the Holy Spirit is mine today.

Joining with the Holy Spirit changes everything.

There are many times throughout a day that we become consumed with resentment or fear or maybe even rage. Any of these feelings indicate that we have been ensnared by the ego. It's also common to believe such feelings are justified. The ego claims to be right, always, regardless of the circumstances.

Our obsession with our feelings is so overwhelming, we can't imagine letting them go. Who would be responsible for "righting" the situation if we backed off? Whew! We do get caught up. We live in fear that if we let go, we'd be lost, we'd be abandoned, we'd have no purpose for living.

How wrong we are, but how gently the *Course* approaches us with an alternative path for living. It offers us the Holy Spirit as guide, comforter, friend, and *controller.* Joining with the Holy Spirit allows us to see every aspect of our lives differently and even makes letting go of all circumstances possible. With just a bit of practice, we can see how safe we are when the Holy Spirit is in control.

All I need is a tiny willingness to let the Holy Spirit make
peace out of the chaos I might create today.

Jesus
Prayer

Prayer can align us with Jesus.

In what terms do we consider Jesus? Based on our religious upbringing, we may consider Jesus far more holy than we have the capacity to be. It's true that Jesus achieved transformation, transcended his body, and gloried only in love for humankind; however, we are promised the same opportunities. Perhaps we can't imagine this personal evolution, but asking for help to suspend our disbelief is the first step in our process.

The idea that we are equal to Jesus, that we are One with Him, may sound sacrilegious. But it's not. It's the most loving way of all to honor Him and us. And becoming aligned with Him allows us to see our experiences as opportunities to forgive and thus love ourselves and then others, just as Jesus did.

Let's remember that Jesus hung on the cross feeling no pain but only forgiveness in His heart for His attackers. This gives us a model to emulate. It won't happen all that easily, no doubt, but it will happen. Praying to the Holy Spirit is the way.

*My prayers will help me today. Whatever I need to see,
I can with the right prayer.*

Seek to know peace, nothing more.

When we're in conflict, we cry out for detailed solutions to our problems. We become apprehensive when we are unable to imagine what the situation needs. We fret and analyze and ask other people's opinions, but we still worry. Generally we assume a complicated answer is necessary.

The *Course* suggests we are making things too hard for ourselves. No matter what we think, we seldom need long, drawn-out solutions. We don't need the collective advice of many people. We don't need to seek one specific answer through prayer. We need peace; within it, miraculously, lie all answers.

The blessing for us is that peace is always available. It's never more than an instant away. In the quiet spaces of our minds, it waits to be called. Searching our minds for complex solutions to daily problems will never provide the answers we deserve. Seeking to know nothing but peace will always satisfy us.

The answers I seek are seldom where I look.
I'll try being quiet today.

The mind is the body's physician.

It's difficult to grasp that the diseased body is actually a reflection of the ego. We resist many *Course* ideas initially. Fortunately, it's not necessary to accept them all simultaneously. We can "try on" *Course* perspectives and observe the difference in how we feel before making the decision to "change our minds."

What we realize before long is that living according to these principles can bring us happiness. We are no longer compelled to focus on the past or other people or what may happen next in our lives. We begin to trust that whatever comes to us is simply an avenue of learning, an opportunity to feel love, forgiveness and peace. And we understand that a health challenge controls us when we think we are only body rather than Spirit.

A fear-filled mind creates a fearful world of experiences. A Holy Mind, one that's listening to the Holy Spirit, knows only peace and joy and love. No adversity blocks the path of the Spirit-filled mind. No condition is anything more than a teaching tool.

I will focus on healing, forgiveness, and love.

We see what we choose to see.

We can't escape responsibility for whatever condition affects us. This isn't the easiest pill to swallow. We learned to blame others in our families of origin for our problems. Now the question we have to ask ourselves is, "Am I happy?" Not many of us would be *here, now,* searching for a better way if our answer was unqualifiably yes. We have not been peaceful, and we have not understood why.

Learning that we are in charge of what we see may sound simple at first. But soon we realize we're "seeing" lots of situations that distress us. Are we really responsible for these too? We know the answer even before we ask it. We can change any situation by wielding a tighter control over our perspective. We'll never see what we are unwilling to see. The converse is also true. If we want joy and peace in our lives, we must create it. No one else can do it for us.

Today is a good day to see my blessings and my opportunities.

Perspective

 *Whatever our experiences, they will
benefit us, and others too, in time.*

When we are overwhelmed by troubles, it's not easy to believe there's a benefit. In the midst of the pain, we're often too distraught to even consider the bright side. That's okay because we're surrounded by friends who can help us see it when we're ready.

Eventually the dreadful experience gets incorporated into our lives. We will profit from it, at some point. And when we share what we learned with others, they will profit too. Nothing is without some meaning. It's also true that no specific circumstance really matters, *in and of itself.* Its purpose has been merely to serve us, to teach us. That's not always easy to understand and harder to accept.

Coming to believe that there is another way to see our lives offers relief. At first we may doubt the soundness of this idea, but trying on a new perspective removes our resistance. Feeling better about our lives is really worth whatever effort it takes.

*I can make a "silk purse" out of whatever happens to me today.
Telling a friend what I learned will help that friend too.*

The ego obstructs our view.

What do we really want to see in the ordinary and extraordinary events of the day? How do we want to feel? So often we forget how the choice is made. No one decides for us, even though we'd like to blame anyone but ourselves for the mood we're in or the bad luck we're having.

If we are feeling angry or depressed, or worse, the ego has gained control of us. The ego takes us as its hostage every time we rely on it. It's far better to acknowledge the ego's presence but then rely, instead, on the Holy Spirit for specific responses to the twists and turns of life. Making this choice changes every detail of every experience we'll have, now and forever.

My view will be clear and full of hope if I turn to the Holy Spirit rather than the ego today.

Oneness

 We are not separate beings. We are all one.

Coming to understand our Oneness with each other changes how we perceive every ripple in a day's happenings. Our problems and our good fortunes take on a different hue. Our Oneness with each other and with God is mysteriously elusive, and the drama we create, again and again, between ourselves and others belies this Oneness.

Some ideas simply must be taken on faith. Our Oneness with all humanity may be one of these ideas. To help ourselves along, perhaps we can acknowledge the similarities we share in our feelings. None of us likes reprimands. Imagined inadequacies haunt each of us. Fear of rejection is not unfamiliar, nor is our interminable obsession of comparing ourselves with our acquaintances. On the other hand, we all enjoy being complimented or appreciated. We all enjoy the satisfaction of overcoming certain obstacles. Seeing how alike we actually are hints at our Oneness, doesn't it?

I will affirm my Oneness with others today.

Remember, we are channels for God's love.

The barriers created to stop the flow of God's love are master-minded by the ego. When we realize this to the fullest extent, we can acknowledge that the ego is not our friend. Its sole purpose is to keep us agitated. We then inflict our agitation onto others, thus giving purpose for the guilt that consumes us.

We don't need this guilt. There is none in the Real World and that's our real home, after all. The lives we seem to be experiencing here are illusory, hard though that is to fathom. Our physical and emotional pain can be gone in the flick of an instant. Pain is nowhere but in our minds, and our minds can be changed.

This feels so mysterious and hard to believe, doesn't it? Why does this life seem so concrete if it isn't? It's helpful to accept that there are some things we may never fully understand. If we can just appreciate that all we need to do is receive the love that God promises us and then pass it on to others, we'll get free of the ego's attachment to us and thus free of our agitation.

I am open to God's love today. Amen.

Thoughts

 Thoughts are everything.

What we see or feel is only what's in the mind because thoughts are everything. We are responsible for our world, of course, and everything in it. Most of us aren't so eager to accept all of that responsibility. The turmoil and "bad luck" can't be our fault every time.

Even though this set of beliefs forces us to give up blaming others, it also empowers us. Our journey to real happiness can be made more quickly when we accept our rightful role. It's really quite fun to realize that we are who we want to be; we think only what we want to think. We can speed up or slow down our journey at will.

The problem is, how do we first understand and then get comfortable with the idea that thoughts are everything? It helps if we share our observations of experiences with others. We'll see how differently each of us catalogues and interprets events. That, in turn, reveals how our thoughts manage us.

I don't need any thought I don't want today.
I'm in charge.

To forgive, to heal, to love is why we're here.

We want to believe there is a grand design for our lives. Many of us believe that God needs us and us alone to handle a particular job. If that brings us peace and security, it's worth believing. But it might be simpler to believe that God just wants us to love each other. According to the *Course*, our careers or the tasks we're working on are not as important as how we treat the people we meet each day.

It is never wrong to do whatever work we're doing to the best of our ability. It may be that no other person can do it quite as successfully. We all hope to end up doing work we can enjoy and that contributes to the well-being of others. But at the very least, we can still contribute to the well-being of others by treating them lovingly.

Believing that we are here, now, for the sole purpose of loving others means we can all do an excellent job, no matter our age, our gender, or race; no matter our present livelihood or our dreams for the future.

Today I can treat others with grace and respect.

JUNE

A miracle is a shift in perception.

We see the machinations in our lives as far more serious and disruptive than they really are. Fortunately, the *Course* is teaching us that a tiny attitude change can result in quite a different experience.

For instance, consider the frustration of getting a flat tire on the way to work. You have been late three times in the past two weeks, and you know your boss will be upset. Initially, you may be convinced the entire day is ruined. You may want to scream at the motorists who don't stop to help or go back home and call in sick. What a perfect opportunity to practice shifting your perception. But how?

The first step is to prevail upon the Holy Spirit, who resides in your mind. Ask for a different vision and then quietly wait while one takes shape. Second, be grateful that the car wasn't thrown out of control when the flat occurred. Third, use the time it takes to change the tire to evaluate the priorities in your life.

Our feelings will be different when our approach to life is. Seeking miracles in this way guarantees them.

I will seek the help I need as often as I need it today.

Giving

Extending love to you heals me.

Too often we hold back, waiting for someone else to give to us before we respond. Simply reacting to life grows tiresome, however. To risk acting first offers us real freedom. Until we try it, we can't imagine how empowering it is.

All of us think we are in a state of need. We think we need more money, more possessions, more beauty, or more friends. If only we had enough, our problems would dissolve. The paradox is that whatever we think we lack is supplied when we give, and so get, more love.

We can heal the lack we feel in only one way: by extending ourselves lovingly, to others. We may hesitate to extend ourselves because we fear we're unworthy of others. What could we possibly have that they'd want?

It's time for suspending our fears and disbelief. It's time for daring to love.

❧

*I yearn to be healed. On any day my soul aches, I can
soothe it by offering love. Today I'll find an opportunity.*

Chaos is self-perpetuated.

We don't easily accept responsibility for the messes in our lives. Because others are seemingly involved, we want to blame them for part of the turmoil. However, the *Course* doesn't let us off the hook. Our experiences are always of our own making, regardless of the people we call perpetrators.

This is not music to our ears when we think we have been victimized. The *Course* says that we receive what we project. But surely we don't desire neglect or worse yet, abuse. How do we explain these behaviors? The *Course* says we project *who* we want; we create *what* we receive. There is actually no one separate from us.

Let's not be discouraged if we can't grasp the meaning of this. The violence around us seems so real. Better that we focus on what we can understand and rest assured that it will make a difference "out there."

Today gives me a chance to project only love. No matter what a circumstance seems to call for, I know love is all that's needed.

Worry
Problems

God has given each of us a special gift.

How often we wake up doubting ourselves depends on how caught we are in the grasp of the ego. Some days going to work seems overwhelming. Handling difficult children or mending fences with a parent gives us fits of anxiety. Obviously we have forgotten the Holy Spirit. We never experience these pangs of uncertainty when we have sought Its help.

If only we could remember that we are exactly where our "services" are needed every single minute. And what are the services? Simply to listen to others with our hearts, and respond with love. No matter where we are or what occupation we have, our task is the same.

We complicate our experiences so much, always trying to figure out the right solution. There is only one solution for everything! We can give up the angst, the need to be right, the worry over outcomes. None of it matters. If we have forgiveness and love in our hearts, we are fulfilling our purpose.

My participation in today's events will reflect the love
the Holy Spirit has given me.

Giving up what we know isn't easy.

Our possessions and friends, jobs and dreams, aren't so easily given up. Not all of them have to go. As we become more willing to experience the depth of the *Course's* teachings, however, and acknowledge the presence of those who have gathered to teach us, we'll realize that changes are happening in our lives, changes we hadn't counted on. Even changes that worry us initially.

Developing trust is a process. We get ample opportunities to practice it. The losses that come to us, the dreams that vanish, the friends who leave are unsettling. These experiences are necessary though. Their time has come and gone. What comes our way now is what we are ready for. Again and again, we have to remind ourselves that there are no accidents. All experiences are meant for our good.

Today I will welcome unexpected experiences.

Healing

Healing occurs when pain has lost its value.

It's common to resist the idea that "those who want to be healed, will be." Are hospitals really full of people who have chosen to be sick? The *Course* says yes.

Accepting responsibility for some experiences is tolerable. For instance, why would we deny that our balance is impaired if we consume too much alcohol, or that running a red light can trigger an accident? However, admitting we're responsible for every aspect of our lives, each joy and every sorrow, is unbearable at first. Fortunately, we don't have to accept and understand overnight how our material world unfolds. Absorbing the news that we do reap what we have sown comes in stages.

But how does this explain healing, or the lack thereof? Monitoring our thoughts about the significant issues as well as the picayune ones enlightens us about our health. If we let the ego determine how we react, we can be certain it will try in some fashion to control the actions and emotions of others. Our "weakened" condition is a tool the ego has valued too often. Laying it aside, for good, will change our health forever.

If my mind is at peace, I will be well today.

What we see is what we get.

We've all had the experience of sharing observations on an event or situation. Some people are able to capture the silver lining every time, regardless of the trauma caused by the situation. And then there's the rest of us!

The exciting news is that every one of us can join the "silver liners" by changing one, tiny habit. We know about the split mind already. That's one of the first lessons taught in the *Course*. All we have to do is link up with the part of the mind marked "Holy Spirit" rather than "ego" to seek our interpretation. Novices though we may be, that's not a difficult assignment, and the results will astound us.

Another word for a better perspective is *faith*. God has never caused harm to us. We may have defined an experience as hurtful, but there always was another way to interpret what was happening. Knowing that each of us can seek a new interpretation, even immediately on the heels of a negative one, softens the sting of an experience.

God will help me see the positive side of life
if I ask for vision.

Holy Spirit

Jesus is our equal.

This may sound like heresy, but Jesus tells us in the *Course* that he was no different than we are now. He merely learned to transcend the ego more quickly than us. The primary lesson for us every day is to call on the Holy Spirit for understanding, a new vision, or merely comfort and guidance. Even when we think we know the best thing to do, we should consult with the Holy Spirit. The ego always has something in mind for us. When we rely on it, trouble is only an act away.

We are not alone, ever. That we often feel alone and scared is evidence that the ego has made us its hostage. However, only the mind has been imprisoned and just for the moment. We can break free by merely thinking of Jesus or God or the Holy Spirit. It's really quite simple, but be aware, the ego will assert itself again. The tug-of-war hasn't ended, but the victor is up to us.

Jesus and I are one. Remembering this will help me handle whatever occurs today.

Both sickness and health are in our control.

We all remember the miracles described in the Bible. Jesus was the healer. It may seem like heresy to claim these healing powers for ourselves now. But the *Course* insists that how we think is tied to how we feel. When we turn our thoughts to peace, our ailments, whether physical, mental, or emotional, will recede.

We are fortunate to have as much control as we have. It's awesome to contemplate how far-reaching our powers are. Knowing that we can use them for our own good, every minute, is refreshing. Remembering to invite the Holy Spirit along for each decision promises a far healthier life.

I am in peak condition if I seek peace and love in my life.

Holy relationships
Unity

Holy relationships await us.

We can't exist without relationships. We mingle with others throughout the day—co-workers, children, spouses, parents, friends. We are thrown together with strangers on the subway, neighbors at the grocery store, and adversaries at company meetings. Since we don't live secluded from others, we have to get along somehow. But how? That's one of our biggest concerns.

The *Course* says there is only one way to get along with others. It's the same formula whether we love or dislike the person. We need to seek a holy perspective of the relationship we share. We need God's help to see that person and ourselves in a circle of light and love. Our feelings will be changed accordingly—every time!

Even the most troubling individual will not disturb our inner peace if we seek to see our coming together as holy. This may sound impossible, or at least improbable, but it's true nonetheless. Testing this idea will dispel our doubts.

Today is a good day for experiments. I will seek the holy
in even the ordinary.

Attacking a problem never results in a solution.

When we think in terms of attacking a problem, we make the problem real. Usually, we incite others to attack us back too. We are learning that a far better approach to life is to go within and ask the Holy Spirit for a more loving perception of every situation that baffles us. It's simple and comforting to live this way.

We can acknowledge this wasn't our path before. We have the battle scars to show for it, but we have learned from our mistakes and we did the best we could with what we knew. How marvelous that we have a more enlightened perspective now. Every experience, no matter how traumatizing initially, will be smoothly incorporated into our lives with the help of the Holy Spirit. Our acceptance of any problem sets a wonderful example for others too. Let's not forget that we are teaching what we have learned all the time. The students are everywhere.

I will teach only love and acceptance today.

June 12

Desires

The Holy Spirit always knows what we need.

Hindsight is a good teacher. Every one of us has been spared our fondest wish on more than one occasion. And today we count our blessings. The marriage we thought we had to have or the job of all jobs would not have brought us lasting happiness. Now we can see what path we were on. It wasn't luck that saved us, although we may have guessed so before coming to the *Course*. Now we know the Holy Spirit was "present" when we were faltering.

There's comfort in the knowledge that the Holy Spirit is always close. But we may wonder why we've experienced some tough times anyway. That's where the ego comes in. Just as we have the voice of the Holy Spirit to rely on, we have the ego's voice at hand. It convinces us far too often to obey its will. The pain and suffering that dot our past are the evidence of its power. Relying on the Holy Spirit rather than the ego will change not only today but also every tomorrow.

I'll meet no trouble today if I listen to the right voice.

Imperfections
Resentment

When others upset us,
we need to look in the mirror.

Every time we resent, or worse, hate, what another person is doing or saying, we need to acknowledge that we are the same. That's not easy. We don't want to own all that we are. In fact, that's the reason we see certain traits in others. We've denied they are our own by pushing them onto someone else and then judging that person. But our denial has now run its course. Adjusting to all that we are and forgiving our imperfections makes it possible for us to honor others with forgiveness too. That's why we are here.

When we willingly see that we are here to understand and cherish forgiveness, we will feel neither fear nor anger when others upset us. We'll simply know that an opportunity to connect with another soul and celebrate our Oneness has presented itself.

School is always in session. At times, this may distress us, but we can be relieved instead. It means we have as many chances and as much time as it takes to grasp all that we are here to learn. What we miss today will come again tomorrow.

Keeping my mirror close by will teach me many things today.

We choose between Truth and illusion every minute.

Why would we choose illusion over Truth? How can illusion hold any interest for us? The explanation is both clear and confusing. The ego, which generally seems to be the "whole" of us, is invested in the illusory world. The ego creates what we see and protects it. The events and the people we experience invite our control; we love and hate this world simultaneously.

To choose Truth means to detach, more or less, from all that we see *here.* We quietly and willingly rise above the chaos in search of inner peace, which is the underlying truth, according to God. But our dilemma is this: How can chaos be ignored when it adversely affects so many? The *Course* reminds us that the ego creates the chaos for its selfish purposes; the Truth lies only within the peace. We can best address the chaos by ignoring it. We can foster meaningful healing by contributing to and acknowledging only peace.

I will look beyond the chaos today and feel only peace.
This will help heal every situation.

We need not die to be in the Real World.

Sorting out the difference between this world we see and the Real World is necessary to understanding the *Course* principles. The notion that the Real World knows no strife, expresses only love, and is the home of God makes it sound like the "Heaven" of our dreams. When we learn that we can be in the Real World in an instant, we're skeptical. How can we be both *here and there?*

It's good that we have all the time we need to understand the elusive points of the *Course.* As Jesus told Helen, the *Course's* scribe, it's a process. For many it will be a long process. And yet, any one of us can get glimpses of how it works every time we willingly change our minds regarding what we think we see.

To experience the Real World, we only need to change our minds, nothing more. The Real World is the home of peace and love, and we can live there at will.

Today is mine to live however I want. If I want to feel
only love, I know what I need to do.

Healed mind

A healed mind is always peaceful.

We have so little patience with ourselves and others. We want perfection, from everybody, in every situation. What should be apparent is that none of us defines perfection in exactly the same way. The result is anxiety, agitation, and struggle. We can't control others, no matter how hard we try or how right we think we are. We are left with only ourselves to control and change and we're not all too eager for that.

What we have is a troubled mind, one that's controlled by the ego. What we need is a mind that functions free of the ego. It's available to us when we take the hand of God, which we have dropped along the way, allowing the ego to capture us. The Holy Spirit is always reaching out to us, but it offers peace, not the assurance of being right. Of course, the ego can't give us that assurance either. When we turn away from the Holy Spirit, it's because we think we need to be right. Being right is not like being peaceful. We can't be both.

Do I really want a healed mind? I'll have many chances today to take the hand of God.

Shifting perceptions changes us completely.

No situation looks quite the same to any two observers. We came to understand this through our willingness to listen to others and surrender the ego's insistence on being right. This is not the same as asking for a different perspective for ourselves, though. And this is what the *Course* suggests we do.

Some of us wonder how this can be. Surely, whatever we see is what is there. Right? Not necessarily. What we see is the absolute reflection of what our hearts are feeling. If it's love we're feeling, we'll see a situation that is hopeful and fulfilling. If it's fear, our vision will be profoundly clouded and our response will be agitated, angry, and full of attack.

We might liken our behavior to having a split personality. Who we appear to be one moment may not resemble who we'll become with a small shift in perception. This tiny act can result in a huge change. We quite likely wish we could have a loving perspective all the time. With a little effort, we can.

I can see however I choose today.
How I act will follow accordingly.

The Course *is one pathway to God.*

It's not unusual to grow up believing that our religious convictions are the only worthy ones. Many churches intentionally indoctrinate parishioners in that way. That's how they maintain control. How refreshing to be told in the *Course* that there are many roads to God. Whatever was our path before need never be denied nor denigrated. It carried us to where we are now. Where we'll go next depends on our desire for additional enlightenment.

We each wish to know God. How exciting to realize we share this journey with so many like-minded people. The trip bonds us; none of us is making it alone, and all of us will arrive. Because we travel together, we are living examples, continuously, of good and poor God-connections. It's not an accident that so many "models" surround us. We'll benefit most from mimicking only those who demonstrate love.

*I seek to know God today. Every encounter
is my opportunity.*

Our minds wander thoughtlessly.

To daydream isn't bad. Some of our most creative ideas come to us when our thinking is unfocused. Let's not relinquish monitoring our thoughts, however, because many of them are not beneficial, particularly when the ego is doing the thinking.

How can we tell who is in charge of our thinking? Perhaps prior to our coming to the *Course,* we never suspected that we had two "personas" behind the curtain of our mind. But it hasn't taken much reflection to see how different we think and behave in some instances than in others. What's going on?

The difference in how we act and think is owing simply to our choice of "thinker." When we let the ego think, we feel only fear and behave accordingly. When we rely on the Holy Spirit, our actions are loving and forgiving. We experience no strife when It's in charge. Why would we ever let the ego speak for us? That's the insanity of this world.

My journey into the Real World beckons today.
I will follow in the steps of the Holy Spirit.

Peace

There is nothing to be afraid of.

It's not easy to internalize the principle that there is nothing to be afraid of. We likely grew up in families where we observed fear firsthand. Now our companions are frequently afraid. So are our children and other loved ones. Fear seems to be a universal emotion. The great news is that it doesn't have to plague us. The remedy is simple. If we're afraid, we've forgotten the presence of the Holy Spirit who is here to protect us and make us peaceful. All we have to do is recall It to memory.

How can we discard fear? Let's practice with small, relatively insignificant experiences. They will be affected by and changed in exactly the same way more serious experiences will be. The routine is this: When a feeling of dread erupts, immediately image the Holy Spirit. Remember that Its assignment from God is to comfort us and bring us peace. Learning, as we will, that we can count on It every time teaches us that we can be free of fear. Forever.

Today can be as peaceful as I want it to be. Even in the face of disaster, the Holy Spirit will give me peace.

Our classroom calls to us every day.

It's comforting to know that we're students on a journey. This means we don't need instant understanding of how this *Course* works and we can forgive our forgetfulness. Every day offers us additional opportunities to use this new information. And each experience promises to teach us new lessons.

When we think about all the events in our lives from this framework, they don't scare us nearly as much. Our trust grows in our ability to learn. We are where we need to be. We can repeat lessons when necessary, and we serve as teachers for those who follow in our tracks.

Defining life as a classroom makes the *Course* principles manageable. We may still feel challenged by the experiences we're having, but we aren't defeated. We are ready for them.

*I will accept whatever comes to me today.
I am a willing student.*

The peace we feel is a measure of our progress.

Many opportunities to call on God for understanding escape us. A power struggle sucks us in so quickly, and the desire to be right is strong. We get on a course of conflict with our friends and even strangers that simply won't let us go. Not one of us sincerely relishes the agitation. But for the moment, we have forgotten that there is another way to experience life.

Perhaps the greatest value of the *Course* study groups is that the members are living examples that there are loving ways to perceive every kind of experience. We can observe group members peacefully accepting circumstances that might drive others crazy. How do they do it? Have they been specially blessed?

Hearing that they have nothing that's not also available to us brings relief, and a measure of doubt. Some situations are too hard for us to imagine being peaceful while we are in them. The important question to ask is, "Do I want a more peaceful life?" If our answer is yes, then we will be shown the way. A little willingness is all we need.

I can have whatever feeling I want every day.

Our interpretation is everything.

The idea that interpretation is everything may seem radical to some. Isn't the automobile crash, the tornado's destruction, the severely handicapped child visible to us all? The answer, of course, is yes. But how we interpret what we observe is the key to what we really see. The material world doesn't tell the whole story.

The real blessing of this new way of thinking is that we can see and respond to whatever picture we choose. The child in the wheelchair smiles because she has just won a race. We can select her happiness as our perspective. The downed trees and devastated mobile park didn't take the lives of ten children who were present when the twister came through. That miracle can claim our attention.

We can respond to every personal encounter as an expression of love or a request for healing and help. How we feel about the moment, the day, each person, our lives will mirror our response to every aspect. The empowerment that flows to us as a result is the real miracle.

I am able to see whatever I really want to see today.
Amid pain and destruction is joy;
it's my assignment to look for it.

June 24

Peace

Our thought system will radically change.

We can probably all remember the first time we picked up *A Course in Miracles.*® Few of us immediately resonated to its message, however. The language may have been too stilted or the sentence structure too confusing to satisfy us. Even worse, perhaps we couldn't understand the message. When someone suggested the content would change how we thought forever, we may have recoiled.

Look at us now. We're convinced life was never more manageable. And that's true. Peacefully we acknowledge others' differences. Quietly we let others have their own opinions. Softly we look upon our experiences knowing that their purpose is our salvation.

Our new way of thinking has changed everything about our lives. To be joyful, peaceful, and spirit-filled every moment is a true possibility. We want to share our good news with others.

Perhaps I will have an opportunity today to help a friend
see his or her life differently.

Loving acts are motivated by the Holy Spirit.

The Holy Spirit is like a special friend with great wisdom and an intense willingness to offer us guidance. It will never lead us astray. Never will we have to make amends if we follow Its lead. Our journey will be filled with acts of kindness, both random and specific, if we let the Holy Spirit plan our trip.

Sometimes the ego wants to get into the "loving" act too. And occasionally, we can trust the voice we hear. However, the ego will push us to offer love for a price. The ego interprets life and love as conditional. The Holy Spirit defines no conditions.

What difference does it make as long as what we do is based on love? Perhaps none in some instances; however, we can't always trust our choices if we have made them impulsively, without first consulting with the Holy Spirit. Its voice is quieter than the ego's, and we have to want to hear it.

*I will show love today following the guidance
of the Holy Spirit.*

Let's pray to get out of the Holy Spirit's way.

Most of us would admit to praying for a better job or more money or secure relationships. It's not wrong to pray for any of these things. However, it keeps us thinking we can control situations if only God answers our prayers. The more we pray, the more willing God becomes, we hope.

Alas, we generally stay stuck because the ego's prayers are so limiting. We only discover this, however, when we let the Holy Spirit take charge of where we go, what we do, what we think, whom we befriend, and thus who we become. We have so much more potential than the ego would ever credit us with.

It's really much easier to pray only to stay out of the Holy Spirit's way. It saves us from needing to figure out what we should do or think in particular situations. It frees us from trying to figure out a friend's life too. There's one thing to do, and only one thing, in every circumstance. Move aside for the Holy Spirit.

I'm tense because I'm trying to control the uncontrollable.
I'll let the Holy Spirit work in my life today.

The ego keeps us stuck.

We keep hearing bad things about the ego. That's not easily understood when we're new to the *Course.* So many other pathways to a better life encourage the development of a healthy ego. How can both be right?

It's really not necessary to debate either viewpoint. Quiet but close observation of past conflicts and the way we struggled within those circumstances will reveal the negative role the ego played in seeking resolution.

It's even possible that the ego might respond to an event almost as the Holy Spirit would. If the ego doesn't feel threatened by a situation, it won't be as invested in controlling the outcome. But we can safely assume that, generally, the ego has a grudge to bear or sees a particular resolution as mandatory. And then we are stuck. Being stuck means we aren't teachable and the growth we deserve doesn't happen.

We have to ask ourselves, Is this what I really want? We can sit and stew about how life *should* be or we can be open to how it *might* be today. Our choice makes all the difference.

I can see conflicts differently today.

**Spirit
Decisions**

Our minds are split.

We have certainly all been confused over making good decisions. Probably we've even said, "I just don't know. I'm torn between two options." The *Course* teaches us how one option frequently reflects the controlling ego, while the other option reflects the Spirit.

The question to ask is, which one feels the best? Thinking we are right and that people should live their lives our way makes us tense, particularly when they don't behave as we'd like, which is often. We aren't eager to admit it, but the ego has caused the tension—not their behavior.

Letting go of people, outcomes, specific plans isn't easy at first. It feels like we are shirking our duty. That's how attached we are to letting the ego hold us hostage. It doesn't feel good though, because every other ego wants its own say too. So we live in perpetual tension.

Since our minds have two parts, why not respond to the world from the Spirit, the side of us that makes us peaceful? It's worth considering, isn't it?

*Both the Spirit and ego beckon today. Only the
Spirit offers me peace of mind.*

Fear may come and go.

Fear visits us when we forget our union with all others and with God. Why is it so hard to remember that we are One, joined for all time with our Creator? It's hard because the ego doesn't want us to remember that. The ego wants us to think we are separate, unequal human beings. The ego wants us to fight with others, to be uneasy with others, to fear the presence of others. The ego is nourished by the insanity that makes us feel separate.

Fortunately, we can turn away from fear every time the ego snares us. Its hold on us is caused by our own unwillingness to ask the Holy Spirit for help, for a different perspective, for even a little awareness of the love that's always present. When the struggle is great, the best we may be able to do is seek some peace a minute at a time. But that's a beginning.

Peace is elusive, but it doesn't have to be. The Holy Spirit is only a tiny thought away. In an instant, we can have the peace and joy we claim to want. This gift awaits us.

I am as free of fear as I want to be every day.
Today beckons.

Happiness

The world does not have to change for me to be happy.

It's not easy to believe that we can be happy if we're in the middle of an unwanted divorce or nursing a terminally ill parent. Rearing children who are out of control is depressing too. Most of us need to look no further than our immediate surroundings to find a reason for unhappiness. It seems like denial when someone tells us the choice to be happy, in spite of circumstances, is easily made.

Looking beyond the contours of the events in our lives is an attainable skill. It doesn't mean our eyes don't see the painful details in this physical realm. Rather, it means we understand that the "material" isn't the actual substance of the spiritual, and it's the spiritual realm we truly seek to know. Our access to this realm lies within our minds. It takes nothing more than the sincere wish to see our circumstances differently to be able to do so. The Holy Spirit is our pathway.

The awful situations that may surround me today cannot hold me hostage. I can be happy if I seek the help of the Holy Spirit.

JULY

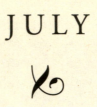

Miracles are merely thoughts.

Whatever our religious background, we've generally thought of miracles as unimaginable outcomes to serious situations, in other words, really big things. Yet the *Course* teaches that miracles are "merely" thoughts. Which is right?

We are learning that miracles can be either. Sometimes a life-threatening health challenge might disappear fully. When that's the case, nobody scoffs; everybody recognizes how big that is. But on the other hand, we have all experienced the unexpected dissipation of an intense power struggle with a colleague and have thought, "What a miracle!"

Miracles are mysterious and elusive. They have no absolute characteristics. The parameters of what defines one changes, depending on the circumstances. But the one element that is the same in all miracles is our change in thinking. Looking at it from this perspective suggests that we can create miracles at will. All we have to do is change our minds.

I can experience a miracle today. The Holy Spirit will help me.

Nothing in this world matters.

The trials of our daily lives—the job loss, the communication breakdown with a spouse, the incorrigible daughter—certainly upset us. How could they not matter?

The *Course* helps us understand that all situations can be interpreted through the eyes of the Holy Spirit. When we call upon It to give us a different perspective, whether on the most traumatic or exceedingly mundane experience, we will feel relief, even peace, in an instant. The understanding we cultivate, in the process, is that, finally, nothing really matters, not when viewed through a holy perspective.

This concept baffles us. We would not be troubled by the idea if we could understand that changing our minds is a decision, a process, a journey, an activity that requires willingness and lots of practice. When we come to grips with this, we're on our way.

My experience today will match my perspective, absolutely.

Seek peacefulness, not specific answers.

Because we think we need to know exactly how to proceed in all areas of life and because we harbor particular wants and desires, we seek complicated, detailed solutions for every situation that surfaces. We muddle our minds with worry over how we should do our part in whatever circumstance beckons. Considering the strength of the ordinary ego, that's not surprising. The ego wants what it wants when it wants it!

There is another way to do our part, however. We can dispense with the idea of detail all together. That may seem unusual but only because we are so accustomed to letting the ego run our lives. Seeking no answer, no solution can be refreshing. Desiring peace rather than a complicated agenda of activities is so much less burdensome. We'll feel like new people, as if a miracle has occurred. And indeed it has. Changing our minds about what to seek changes everything about what we get.

What I seek, I will find. I will quietly remember this today.

Oneness
Equality

All people are equal.

The ego gleefully makes us feel inadequate to others. We can't forget that the ego's only hold on us is in making us feel fearful, less than adequate to the tasks and the people around us. Refusing to accept this as our reality, takes both Herculean strength and the humility to look to the Holy Spirit for a different perception of ourselves.

While we are all equal, we each have different personalities, unique strengths and weaknesses, and specific dreams and abilities. It's easier to accept our complexities when we remember that every one of us is needed to make the Whole. We all bring something vital to the "party."

When we believe in our equality, we are less threatened and more peaceful. The next step then to accepting that *we are all One,* is not so far removed from our understanding. When we understand our Oneness, we are home.

I am as I need to be. I am neither better
nor worse than my companions.
I am their equal in every way today.

Be still.

Often, we grudgingly and hurriedly move from one activity to the next, feeling out of time and short of breath. Is there really that much to do? Some of us keep ourselves busy in order to feel worthwhile. If that's the case, let's remember that it's the ego, not our real self, that perceives lack of worth. We simply need a change of mind, now, and then we can rest. The stillness awaits us. In the stillness we heal.

Beginning each day with a time of stillness gives us a chance to remember the Holy Spirit. That's no guarantee that we will not be ruled by the ego in the next hour, but each recollection makes the next one easier. Practice makes it natural to turn to the Holy Spirit for the guidance and the peace we deserve.

We need not be busy all the time. We need not be busy ever, in fact. It's our choice to be peaceful or busy. We'll do a better job of the former if we have been still for a few moments.

*Going peacefully through today
is easiest if I've had some
quiet time with the Holy Spirit.*

Pain has only one cause.

Most times we feel surrounded by signs of pain. The media inform us that children, worldwide, are starving. Signs of political strife are evident in most countries. Senseless, random violence strikes even the most protected neighborhoods. The signs of pain are multiplying. How can there be only one cause?

The *Course* tells us that fear causes pain because fear triggers attack, in some form, on whomever is close. It's neither logical nor defendable. As we understand fear, its cause and its consequences, we can seek its alternative, love.

If the idea of holding only loving thoughts seems unattainable, it's because we haven't tried it. It's doable. It's also the only antidote to the painful conditions throughout the world. Realistically, none of us can change the experiences of every living person, but each of us can change the experiences of all those whom we touch. And that's the beginning of the end of pain.

I will make a contribution on behalf of love today.
My example will influence someone else too.

Let's teach acceptance.

Nothing has the absolute power to control us or destroy us. We may fold under the hostile criticisms of strangers or be daunted by the outrageous actions of friends, but we always have another available response. It's this: We can see every person, no matter who they are, as the Teachers we're ready for. This doesn't mean we won't feel their insults. Nor does it mean we won't resist their lessons. It simply means we can learn to be detached from the particulars of the situation, focusing instead on the opportunity to accept and love even that which injures the ego.

Acceptance isn't as difficult as we may think. Actually, it's a simple decision that bears repeating, as often as necessary. When we choose to accept an experience as a learning opportunity, regardless of its nature, it profoundly changes the tenor of our journey. We're often reminded that the sticky details of our experiences don't matter. Why don't we relinquish our resistance to this idea?

I will accept today's journey as the one I'm ready for.

July 8

Choice
Perspective

Two thought systems forever beckon.

We have two options for interpreting every experience in our lives. We can perceive ourselves as victims of innumerable forms of continual attack or we can see only expressions of love. The latter thought system is generally the more difficult.

Being the brunt of a friend's angry outbursts or the employee who gets laid off makes perceiving only love challenging. And our struggle is heightened because the ego is so invested in "this world," even though we are told this world we see isn't the Real World, it is our classroom. It does exist in the sense that we are here to learn how to live unencumbered by this material realm.

There will be times when we choose to feel pity for ourselves. We may strike back at others, victimizing them for revenge. This negative, narrow, hateful thought system wins us over too often. But as long as we occasionally experience the fruits of expressing only love, we'll cultivate the desire to return again to this thought system. Our lives will reflect the difference.

I can lean one of two ways when perceiving
this next twenty-four hours. Defining each
experience as "good" will benefit me the most.

We are not who we see in the mirror.

If we're not who we see in the mirror, who are we? And where are we? Certainly everything in the world we touch reinforces our mirror image. Our interactions with others, our dreams and failures, our successes and accidents belie that we're not here. Learning that our image is solely the ego's selfish creation and not real seems like nonsense. Our wariness is great. How can we be certain?

Because we are hostage to this world, it's hard to fathom that it is illusory. It's equally hard to understand that time isn't real. We can certainly remember getting up this morning. We can recall our graduation from college and the birth of a child. We are planning a midwinter vacation. How can time not exist?

All that we may have believed before now is being tossed aside, and it makes us uneasy. We aren't required to understand, instantly, what the Real World is. All we need to do for now is accept that what we think we see isn't what's really there. The Holy Spirit is our pathway to understanding.

*I'll need the Holy Spirit today. Without Its voice,
I'll lose sight of what's for my good.*

Special relationships

Our substitutes for God are everywhere.

Because we mistakenly think God has abandoned us, we feel an awful emptiness within. In our search to feel better, we clutch at other people, forcing "special" relationships, hoping that their presence in our lives will fill us up. Our attempts are unnecessary. God never left us. It's we who moved. It's we who will have to reconnect with God. We are capable of doing that right now. All that's necessary is the desire and the decision to go quietly within.

Why do special relationships seem so attractive? They cause us frequent pain, and the feeling of abandonment visits us often. What also accompanies these relationships is an occasional moment of seeming control over someone else, thus our future. When we're feeling this, we're certain we'll never be rejected again. But that feeling is extremely short-lived. We can't, finally, control someone else. And when this person leaves, we seek another substitute then another and another. Let's seek God instead.

Why settle for a substitute for God today?
The real thing is as close as my mind.

Problems are not as we see them.

Our perspective determines our interpretation of an experience. What amuses one person may anger a second and edify a third. Thus we may wonder how we are ever to get along with other people. Differing perspectives give rise to simple disagreement, major dysfunction, and at the extreme, violence and war. We see the evidence everywhere.

So what does it mean to say problems are not as we see them? Well, if we realize that each person sees each situation differently we begin to see that no problem is definite or absolute in scope. It is possible to see problems from a different perspective if we're willing to stretch our minds.

How do we stretch our minds? It's rather easy. We go to the quiet space within for a different view of that which troubles us. If our request is sincere, and our willingness genuine, we'll find that which we seek.

*If I don't like what I see today, it's up
to me to seek a different view.*

Forgiveness heals.

We can contemplate forgiveness on many levels. We suffer from guilt, thinking that if others knew who we really were, they would abandon us. We also feel guilty about our judgments of others. According to the *Course,* we carry an additional, internal guilt because we separated from God, thus leaving the Real World. And worse yet, we created this nightmare we're living.

When we factor into this formula that we are all One, the question of who needs forgiveness becomes even more complicated. Our Teachers suggest it's we ourselves, primarily, who need to be forgiven. The other people in our lives are merely filling the roles we've devised for them.

This may seem confusing, but remember, there are only two expressions anyone can make: the offer of love or the cry for healing and help. If we aren't doing the former, we're doing the latter and forgiveness is called for. To heal is our lesson, to teach it and to learn it.

I may need to forgive someone today.
My offer of love will do it.

God created only Spirit.

Most of us grew up believing that God made everything. We felt secure thinking that the trees, the oceans, the creatures galore, and all human life were the direct creations of an all-powerful God. That interpretation certainly didn't hurt us; however, we are learning now that God isn't the creator of the world we see. In fact, it doesn't even exist in God's realm.

This news is unsettling at first. We wonder: Can so many religious beliefs be wrong? Fortunately, we don't have to defend this principle to anyone. Deciding to believe it and then adjusting how we live our own lives will exemplify the value of this belief to anyone who really cares.

What does this principle do for us? For one, it makes us take responsibility for how we see the experiences in our lives. Further, it convinces us that we'll only see what we have chosen to see. Coming to believe that the ego causes our consternation gives us the freedom and encouragement to make other choices. Knowing that we created our messes humbles us. It can also empower us.

*I create the smooth flow of my life today.
The rocky road is my creation too.*

Belief in separation causes every problem.

Is it possible to think of ourselves as a single, unified whole with others? Every encounter we have feels like we are separate minds and separate bodies. In particular, the differing opinions that emerge about every experience substantiates this notion. But this is so only because we have chosen to believe we are separate, rather than One. If this belief doesn't serve us well, why do we cling to it?

Our teachers would tell us that separation is a trick of the ego. It keeps us stuck and at odds with one another. In one mad moment, the mind devised the separation and this world of conflict. Our task is to return to the Real World where we are peacefully One, even now.

How do we get there? Make the decision to go. It's that simple. Look upon your brothers and your sisters as extensions of yourself, and only that, and you will have arrived.

*My problems exist only in my mind.
Today I can feel peace.*

To join with another is to heal.

The need for healing implies a state of sickness, of disease. If we think of this state in terms of disease, we'll understand it better within the context of the *Course*. We experience *dis-ease* every time we imagine ourselves as separate minds and separate bodies in competition for the material possessions of this illusory world. To want, to grab, to hide what we have from one another in order to secure it is the root of our inner turmoil. That, in turn, is the root of our illness.

To join with others is a holy connection. It's an explicit blending of minds, thoughts, opinions, possessions. Truly joining with another, any other, is love in its purest state. Through this state of total acceptance and sharing we experience emotional, mental, and physical healing.

Our lesson is to heal. And to help one another heal too. It happens in a moment, a tiny moment. As one heals, we all heal. It begins with love, even the smallest expression of love.

I can be the one who offers healing today.
Giving love is the way.

Peace

We can give up what our eyes see.

One of the earliest exercises in the *Course* workbook tells us that nothing we see is real. It's not easy to grasp this idea. Our leg hurts when we bump it; the chair moves when we sit on it; the plate breaks when we drop it. What can it possibly mean that "what we see isn't real"?

Clarity comes when we recall the text telling us that Jesus looked upon his wounds but did not see them. He looked beyond them and saw, instead, the crucifiers' fear and forgave them. Perhaps we aren't yet able to respond so nobly to the many adverse conditions in our lives; however, we, too, can look past them if we so desire. But how?

The method is the same in every instance. When we're distressed about anything at all, seek another perspective from the Spirit within. This response doesn't make circumstances vanish. We may still see the turmoil, but we have no need to react to it. Peace has come, instead. It will always come if we seek it.

What captures my attention is my responsibility today.
I will see what I choose to see.

We can look at problems differently.

How do you look at the loss of a job differently? Or a stalled car or an angry spouse? Problems are problems!

When first told that we can see even the most horrendous of circumstances differently, we may suspect it means being in denial. Therapists and friends have warned us against denial. We'd stay stuck in our problems, they claim. Thus it's easy to be leery of the *Course*'s teachings at first. Being assertive means taking care of ourselves, we've been told. Surely we aren't supposed to quit doing that!

In this regard, the main lesson of the *Course* seems radical. It asks us to willingly seek another view of whatever situation is distressing us, even if we are being hurt. That's a bold request, and it's natural to resist it at first. Those among us who have tried seem so happy though. Could it be . . . ?

*It can't hurt me to try to see my circumstances differently.
I owe myself this opportunity today.*

July 18

Relationships

  Lifelong relationships aren't always smooth.

It's common for individuals to discard relationships that aren't pleasant. In terms of the *Course,* however, we are attracted to learning partners by design. Leaving a hostile relationship probably means working out that same struggle with someone else, some other time. It's not wrong to decide to leave, but let's not assume there's no lesson in every encounter.

Looking at relationships from this perspective removes the fear about them. Acknowledging that conflict is due to the ego's selfishness makes it possible to understand its attempt to control. We come to believe that we need not get along beautifully every minute of the day for a relationship to be lifelong and meaningful. The desire to join as One in spirit and love rather than fight as separate, hateful human beings is reason enough to open our hands to the Holy Spirit each time some tension ensues.

I don't have to be happy every minute to stay in a relationship.
I will take note of the opportunities to see
beyond the struggles today.

*Asking to see as Jesus would see
is our sole responsibility.*

It's amazing how simple our lives can be if we do what the *Course* suggests. How many times a day do we wring our hands in worry over what action to take? How often do we lash out at a friend or speak rudely to a stranger because we are obsessed with fear about our lives? There would be no stumbling blocks if we'd go to the source of all right answers, all right guidance. But Jesus will wait for us, we are told.

If all we have to do is ask Jesus for a better view, why do we struggle so long? It seems crazy to think we like the turmoil, but we can get so used to the agitation that it feels safe. Familiar pain may seem more comfortable than unfamiliar stillness. It behooves us to notice those people in our lives who are serene, who radiate a calm love and acceptance of both the joys and the upheavals in their lives. It's probable that they have sought the right answer from the right source. We can follow their lead.

*I will ask to see my options from Jesus'
perspective today.*

Honesty

 Honesty inspires peacefulness.

We all desire peace, but we don't always practice peacefulness. We may argue or pout. We may plot to control or confuse others. We may even engage in sinister activities. But the fact of the matter is, we'd rather be at peace. We just aren't very good at accomplishing it.

Making the decision to be lovingly honest is the key to peacefulness. How do we do it? It's not difficult, but it does require that we acknowledge how quickly the ego interferes in our lives. The ego has a vested interest in our dishonesty. If the ego is in control, and that's always its intent, it stops at nothing to stay in control. Taking into account what may be the best outcome for everyone concerned is never of interest to the ego. The ego seeks self-gratification only. Peace doesn't live there.

Asking for help from the Holy Spirit is the only way to develop real honesty. It can be immediate but most of us will have to ask many times. In fact, we'll have to first be willing to ask. Let's not give up.

The opportunity to be honest, thus peaceful, will present itself many times today.

Giving

To give and receive are one.

Life's paradoxes confuse us less as we mature. We begin to understand that giving and receiving result in even exchanges. Much of society may still assume that what one gives away is gone forever, but we know differently. How refreshing to function with this awareness. We'll never be empty-handed again.

Opportunities for giving are everywhere. We may not always recognize them, however, because far too many come as angry attacks or subtle put-downs. It's probably safe to say that situations in which our giving is most needed will rarely appear as pleasant opportunities. Rising above each circumstance in order to see God within it will become second nature to us in time. The more we are able to give, unconditionally, the greater our own rewards will be.

Miracles are just waiting to happen. Through adopting the *Course* principles as guidelines for living, we become privy to the miracle of peace in every daily encounter. Most of us never imagined life could be so rich. Let's do our part today.

*I can contribute good to someone else's
life today by being full of love.*

July 22

Insanity

Insanity is seductive.

Surely people don't find insanity desirable. But careful observation of how others react to their lives and an honest appraisal of how we sometimes act suggest otherwise. Perhaps we're lacking a clear definition of insanity. What does it look like?

Insanity wears many faces. It might be said that there are as many examples of it as there are people in this world. Anytime we listen to the voice of the ego, following its suggestion rather than that of the Holy Spirit, we engage in insane behavior. The most obvious demonstration of insanity is the incessant attempt to control other people; we're all guilty of this.

The most horrendous acts that people commit are easily labeled insanity. The tiny, mean-spirited treatment we're all capable of is just as insane, according to *Course* teaching, but so easily overlooked. We'll make real progress on our journey when we can acknowledge that every time we turn away from the Holy Spirit's voice is a moment of insanity.

My willingness to seek the Holy Spirit's guidance in all matters today determines how sane my actions will be.

Let's bring the ego to the Holy Spirit.

Is the ego always the culprit when troubling circumstances occur?
Not necessarily. But if we're not directing a loving act, the ego has
likely assumed the lead in our "drama." How can we alter the situations that threaten to doom us? By bringing our troubled selves,
our tortured expressions to the Light within. Any consternation
we feel, any angst or anger or fear that controls us, will be melted
away as though it never existed when we are bathed in the Light
of the Holy Spirit.

Even though we know this is true, there are moments we
can't fathom the power the Holy Spirit so quietly wields. If the
ego's hold is finally that tenuous, how does it catch us at all? That
possibly is the greatest mystery of our human journey.

Going to the Holy Spirit, again and again, doesn't lessen our
welcome. We're never like the guest who stayed too long. The
more we visit the Light, the more clarity we'll accumulate and the
more peaceful we'll become.

I seek understanding and I know where to look today.

Peace

 Inner peace isn't related to outer circumstances.

Typically, whatever series of events occurs or is expected to occur over the next few hours of the day influences how we'll feel about ourselves, about the men and women joining us today, about the potential for a successful outcome regardless of the endeavor. It seems not only reasonable but tacit to plan accordingly. After all, don't causes have their effects?

Not so, says Jesus, in the *Course*. They are one. Whatever is happening on the material plane has no authentic connection to the inner spiritual plane. The ego may tie them together momentarily, but then, we're no longer reflecting the Spirit's point of view. The ego is calling the shots.

It's a wonderful piece of news that no matter how dire the circumstance, we can function unruffled. It's possible to master this approach to life. Perhaps it's our assignment to be the "way shower."

I am as peaceful as I want to be today. Nothing that happens has to interfere with this.

The ego knows no truth.

Where do we find the Truth? Many think they have it. Most would not knowingly steer us wrong; however, the only certainty we have of getting the truth is if we ask the single Source that knows Truth: the Holy Spirit. We can access the guidance of the Holy Spirit if we quiet ourselves and listen. We must be still and patient. The ego, the loud one we'll hear ever so quickly, is seldom the right one. Listening takes practice.

The ego wants my attention every minute. I can ignore it today and seek the Truth instead.

Separation

 Everything is simple in the Real World.

Considering how daunting and painful some of our experiences are, we wonder why we remain here rather than returning to the Real World. Even more, we wonder why we came here at all. There is an explanation. We are here because in one tiny, mad moment the ego saw its chance for power and split off from God. It has fought to maintain its control ever since. However, God didn't forsake us. When the imagined separation occurred, the Holy Spirit became our companion to smooth our journey and to guide us back to the Real World when we are ready. What's taking us so long?

The truth is that we can go to the Real World whenever we want. It's not a place of bricks and mortar. We don't need travel plans to get there. The decision to express and receive only love from all our compatriots transports us to the Real World in an instant. There is no strife there. Peace and joy are permanent residents. We can remain "there" too.

My attitude is all that keeps me from the peace of the Real World. I can make the trip there today in an instant.

Helping others is always right.

Whenever we extend the hand of friendship to someone else, we are befriending ourselves as well. We aren't separate minds and separate bodies. We only think we are. And we will grow in our understanding of our connectedness as we absorb the benefits of our kindnesses to others. What we offer comes back to us. In reality, it never even leaves us. Each of us heals as others are healed.

Knowing that we share the same journey as the men and women we meet each day removes the threat of their presence. This doesn't mean that every person will treat us kindly or respect our opinions. Each of us struggles between listening to the ego and letting the voice of God decide our path, our actions, our thoughts. But knowing how similar we are to others removes the fear we harbor.

Seeing our own fear reminds us that our fellow travelers have it too. Helping them feel more comfortable is today's assignment.

I will take every opportunity to ease another's load today.

Truth

Only God is real.

Considering the fact that we can't see God, but we can see each other, our bodies, our towns, our possessions, it's not easy to grasp that all but God are illusory. The opposite seems to be true. What then comprises all that we "think we see"?

The *Course* teaches that the ego is the creator of the entire material world. This suggests that the ego works long hours! Indeed, it ceaselessly works to keep us agitated and ready to attack and be attacked. Its power lies in our unending, haunting uncertainty about all our experiences. Reading in the *Course* that nothing is real but God makes us feel crazy at times. How do we intelligently explain all the people, places, and things we can touch?

Maybe we don't need to explain anything. Perhaps that's a radical notion, but contemplating it, for a moment, offers a hint of peace. Can't we accept some things on faith? If nothing we see is real, can it really harm us?

No matter what transpires in my life today,
I'll savor the Truth that nothing is real but God.

Let's begin where we are.

We're seeking to understand our purpose here. We're told this world is our classroom. Does the pain and confusion we feel much of the time mean we're deserving of punishment? Of course not, but the guilt comes so naturally to us; it's difficult to shake these fears about ourselves. It's comforting to hear that we're always where we need to be even when we don't understand what this means.

Our return to God, which is the intent of our journey, is our ultimate destination. Every one of us has this same destination, the same, underlying purpose here. However, we all take steps, learn specifics, encounter experiences that are unique to only us. And we have to pass through the circumstances that call to us when the time is right, when our time has come.

We may not be able to account for many situations today. They won't seem to fit with what happened yesterday. The best attitude to cultivate is one of gentle indifference. We are where we are needed. We'll arrive when our journey is done.

I need not think beyond the next moment.
Today is taken care of.

Worry

 We can choose to have no cares,
no worries, no anxieties.

This seems like a frivolous wish. To believe that it's a choice seems highly improbable. How can we not worry about our children, marriages, and jobs? To believe we want to worry seems ridiculous, but that's the truth. Many don't accept this idea quickly, but we all will if we follow the suggestion offered in the *Course*.

This suggestion is so simple, so tiny, and so subtle that it doesn't seem like it could affect anything. At first it seems like we're in denial about our problems, but we're in for a big and pleasant surprise. The *Course* says, think and act with the help of the Holy Spirit. Regardless of what the ego tells us, we can see ourselves joined with "the adversaries." We can see their anger or attack or control as a request for healing and help, nothing more. We can answer them with love. Nothing more. And our lives will change forever.

I'll make whatever choice I want to make today.
Worries don't just happen.

Projection

What kind of people surround us?

Some days it seems like we're confronted by difficult, demanding people. Nothing we do satisfies them. The more irritated we get, as a result, the more conflict we engender. This cycle intensifies quickly.

If we're lucky, a friend reminds us that what we see and who we attract are what we have projected. We hate hearing this because we resist being responsible for what we reap in this life. Fortunately, our friends don't shut up, nor do they go away. They, too, are our projections; they represent our better self whose voice is still soft.

We can be grateful that we have influence over who we travel with. We get whoever we are! This information immediately clarifies what needs to change minute by minute.

Today I'll see what I need to do by who is present.

AUGUST

Miracles undo the ego's work.

We were likely raised to think we needed a strong ego. Self-help books extol the benefits of knowing yourself, asserting yourself, willfully taking charge of your life in even the tiniest of details. That advice is not necessarily bad; however, when our actions have injured someone, physically or emotionally, we need the "miracle" of taking action in a new way. We have to be willing to let the ego go in order for that to happen.

How do we let the ego go, particularly after we have spent years trying to develop a "healthy" one? The *Course* would suggest that there is no healthy ego. Its very nature is to be in control of people, situations, and experiences, and doing so exacts a great price from the peace that could be available to all. As students of the *Course,* let's accept that this is true and seek the miracle of seeing any situation in another way.

The ego starts arguments so easily, so thoughtlessly. We want our own way. We forget we are One and there's only one way. Let's decide to remember.

I will remember we are One today.
Seeing anew won't be so hard.

*A single instant of loving without attack
heals our minds.*

Our minds are always choosing between giving love or criticism to whomever is close, and the repercussions of our choices far outlast the choices themselves. The peace and joy or worry and sickness we experience are directly proportional to it.

Considering how easily we can elevate the tenor of our lives thus our health too, why would we ever attack a companion? Attack will always adversely affect us, the attacker. Common sense would suggest that we'd avoid attack at all cost. The ego, the attacker, is not rational, however. It chooses to see everyone as a potential enemy and assumes it had better get the upperhand quickly. There is never a moment's peace when the ego speaks.

The mind is healed when it expresses love. It experiences nothing but genuine peace when it chooses to feel love. The decision to love can be made and remade a thousand times a day, and every time we choose love, we add to the healing of everyone else.

*My mind is as peaceful and as healed as my willingness to
give only love to all my companions today.*

*Pleasure and pain are the same because they
are about the body.*

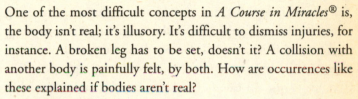

One of the most difficult concepts in *A Course in Miracles*® is,
the body isn't real; it's illusory. It's difficult to dismiss injuries, for
instance. A broken leg has to be set, doesn't it? A collision with
another body is painfully felt, by both. How are occurrences like
these explained if bodies aren't real?

Enlightened students of the *Course* understand that bodies are
not real in the ultimate explanation of life, but they do serve as our
vehicles for moving through this experience. What we can develop,
however, is the willingness to see beyond the body and feel no pain
related to it. Jesus, while on the cross, served as our role model.

The question facing us is, "Why would we want to ignore
injuries?" The answer is, "Nothing worthy is gained by acknowledging them." When we focus on our injuries, we are honoring
the ego, and it is not serving us. It's creating our battles in fact.

Let's not fret too much if this concept baffles us. Putting our
focus, instead, on simply seeing whatever the Holy Spirit wants
us to see will give us our necessary answers.

*My body is an extension of the ego. It will not hinder me in
any way if I stay attuned to the Holy Spirit today.*

Turmoil

 Nothing in this world means anything.

The pain of living—the injured child, the broken heart, the dying parent—feels very significant. Yet the *Course* says that everything in this world is meaningless. Do our lives, then, mean nothing? What the *Course* is trying to tell us is that in our separation from God, *we created this world of problems.* It didn't create us, and in the Real World, from whence we came and to where we'll return, there remains only God and love. In that world we are composed of both. And in that world we can continue to live if that's our choice.

Practically speaking, though, we are here in these bodies for the moment, which means we have to acknowledge the other bodies around us. We can look upon them acceptingly, knowing that the details we see are up to us. Asking the Holy Spirit to help us see them as they really are will relieve us of the burden of trying to make them different or better.

It's not easy to explain to a stranger of the *Course* how our view of the world is changing. But it is. We feel it, and it feels good.

I don't need to react to the turmoil around me today. If I put my focus on peace and love, the turmoil will leave.

We are instruments for learning and teaching.

The ego made our bodies, which reflect the physical and mental limitations of our imagination. From the Holy Spirit's perspective, our bodies are perfect. And from God's perspective, they don't even exist. The contemplation of these "realities" explains some of our confusion. When we look at ourselves from our Right Mind, we see a far different picture than the one which so commonly troubles us.

If we can consider our bodies as simply vehicles for learning from one another, and thus teaching one another, we will not place so much importance on how they look. Rather, we will focus on what they reveal. Understanding that they do have a bigger purpose frees us from our obsession with how they look, or how we think they should look.

Understanding that we have come here to remember what we need to know to return to our home with God reduces the anxiety we feel over the many situations that confound us. Our experiences are our lessons. They are to be noticed, accepted, and forgiven if hurtful. Not judged. We can't fail the *Course* if we trust the voice within.

*Today I'm in school. May the Holy Spirit
help me be willing to learn.*

Conflict

The ego doesn't love.

We are more than the ego, fortunately. While in the midst of a conflict, it may seem otherwise, but that's because the ego is so loud, so demanding. It gets our attention all too quickly, and then we're trapped in whatever tug-of-war it created. There is no negotiation when the ego is in charge of our thoughts and actions.

Our split mind can come to the rescue. We never have to experience conflict; every situation can be negotiated. We simply have to seek the part of ourselves that wants this—the Holy Spirit. It's as close as the ego. That's the good news. The bad news is that we have to be more intent on hearing Its remarks if we want something different in our lives.

Everyone wants to be loved, not attacked. We'll be treated respectfully and lovingly by approaching others in this manner. When we attack, we can expect the same. But if we're attacked, let's choose to love, instead. It will change the entire experience. It will ultimately change the human race.

The ego doesn't befriend me or anyone else. If I want this day to be pleasant, I'll rely on the Holy Spirit.

Our agitation can easily be dissolved.

The tension of agitation exhilarates us on occasion. We may even like the feeling. Its outcome seldom satisfies us, however. Being at odds with others frequently escalates tension beyond our tolerance level. And then what?

The short-term gratification we may get from cursory agitation doesn't feel good for long. So often we feel stuck with it, but that's never actually the case. We can be free of it instantly. We can just as quickly grab it back, of course.

The challenge of finding a peaceful path seems overwhelming many days. It's interesting that we find it harder to choose peace rather than turmoil. Only when we understand how insistent and persistent the ego is about controlling us can we in turn fathom the seriousness of our struggle. The ego never has to win, however. That's up to us.

I will be at peace today if that's my choice.

Sanity

*We can always perceive sanity
in the most insane people.*

Serial killers, child abusers, rapists seem way beyond the reaches of sanity. Surely they can't commit their horrendous crimes if there's an ounce of sanity in them. So why are we told to look for the sanity?

The *Course* says that even the most destructive person is God and thus can't be evil or insane. How does one explain the violence reported in the news then?

Once again, we are reminded that we have a split mind; we are governed by one side or the other, the ego or the Holy Spirit. When an act of violence, covert or overt, is committed by anyone, the ego is the culprit. When the Holy Spirit acts, all is peaceful. Let's remember that the potential for peace is always present, even when an act of violence is occurring. By looking for it, we can nurture it.

*I'll always look for the peaceful side of
everyone. If that's my focus today, I'll make
a worthy contribution to humanity.*

To heal the mind is to heal the body.

As students of the *Course,* we must guard against putting ourselves down when we manifest illness of any kind. While it's true that "right-mindedness" can prevent sickness, we are merely students, not avatars, and we're still learning about our mind's power as we travel this path. It's an exciting journey, and every experience offers us another piece of the puzzle we're creating. Let's nurture gratefulness.

Our doubts and misperceptions, normal in any learning process, trigger the aches and pains we experience. Simply acknowledging this and then allowing our minds to change will, in turn, change what the body feels. It's not always easy to let the mind change, because the ego is invested in maintaining control of our minds. Fortunately, the ego doesn't occupy the whole mind. The Holy Spirit is present too. When we think with the Holy Spirit's help, our aches and pains remarkably diminish.

*How I think affects how I feel. My health will reflect
how I'm thinking today.*

Thoughts
Right thinking

We can "correct" our thoughts.

Knowing that we can change our thoughts releases us from the hold any negative idea or opinion has over us. We have all heard someone lament, "I can't help how I think. It's just who I am." On the contrary, says the *Course,* we are the creators of our thoughts. We are responsible for who we are. What's good about this is that it means we can change a situation instantly by changing how we perceive it.

Some thoughts are obviously not good for us—the plan to inflict harm on someone because we aren't getting our way, for instance. Others are much more subtle, such as wishing bad luck on a friend. These thoughts might not manifest themselves in others' lives, but they do affect ours. The guilt we accumulate hinders us in all relationships. This in turn changes every experience we have.

Learning, as we presently are, that thoughts can be changed instantly gives us the tool for the kind of holy experience we truly deserve.

I will choose my thoughts wisely today. If I'm uncertain, the Holy Spirit is available for consultation.

Giving love reinforces it.

Most of the agitation any of us feel stems from the belief that we aren't getting what we want and think we deserve. More money, more possessions, more friends, more love, more happiness. Seldom do we focus on what we may be giving to others; rather, we notice what they aren't giving to us!

It's true that some people will always have more material wealth than us and others will have less. However, when it comes to peace of mind, we may selfishly hang on to what we think makes us happy—a relationship or our job status—fearing its disappearance. The paradox is that we do lose what we so stingily hang on to.

It's a radical change of perspective to focus on what we give. We are so used to assessing what we are given, and we judge a person's value accordingly. None of us would deny that we'd like more peace and love in our lives. That's easy to decide. The reality is that we can get exactly that as quick as a flash. All we have to do is give away what we want. It will come back to us.

What I get today I have asked for by my actions.

Sins

Because we think sin is real,
forgiveness is impossible.

We struggle to understand the truth about sin. How can rape or murder not be real? We've all felt the brunt of someone's attack, haven't we? What we're learning, some of us more quickly than others, is that our perception of all experiences reflects our projection. When we think someone has injured us, we have to examine our thought systems. If the ego is controlling what we experience, we'll seldom know peace-filled, joyful times.

The *Course* says that in the Real World, forgiveness is never necessary because sin does not exist. In that world, all are One with God, which means no wrong can ever be done. The paradox, of course, is that we're still in the Real World although we don't realize it. Therefore, sin can't really exist because this world doesn't really exist. Although true, this can be confusing when we're initiates to the *Course*. It's helpful to bring our perceived sins to the light of the Holy Spirit. With God's help, we'll see these sins melt away and forgiveness will fill our hearts.

If I think I'm wronged today, I'll take my thoughts to
the Holy Spirit for reinterpretation.

We share all traits that we note in others.

Few of us are content with every one of our characteristics. For example, we may appreciate our capacity to feel compassion for others and detest that we aren't good at tennis. Our physical appearance may satisfy us, while our struggle to figure out a new computer program embarrasses us. We simply aren't everything the ego would like us to be. The same can be said for all our companions.

This *Course* offers us a process for strengthening those traits we are proud of. It suggests that the qualities we note in others, we always share. And when we want to improve certain positive traits, we should watch intently for them in others. Noting only the positive qualities lessens our own negative ones. This is a principle that always holds true. Of course, the converse is also true. Let's be careful about what we focus on in others. It will determine who we eventually become.

If I want to magnify a certain personality trait today, I can help the process by seeking it out in my friends.

August 14

Healing

 We heal this world when we heal our minds.

There is no sickness in the Real World. It can only be created in this illusory world by minds that listen to the ego instead of the Holy Spirit. The effort required to be free of illness is actually very small. Moment by moment we can choose to be guided by the ego or the Holy Spirit. The health and well-being of everyone is directly affected.

Accepting the challenge to heal the world is daunting initially, because we have struggled unsuccessfully to change the behavior of a spouse or maybe a child. Exerting our will on the likes of another person simply can't succeed, not for long anyway. It's natural that we'll doubt we can effect any change in the bigger world. Putting our doubts aside takes willingness. Fortunately, we have the example of others in our study groups. If they could change their minds, we can do the same, at this moment.

❤

Because I interact with others all the time, I have the opportunity to spread wellness around.

Disturbing situations will no longer exist.

At first it seems like we're in denial to believe that nothing has to disturb us. Broken marriages are upsetting. Job loss, theft, or physical violence can't be ignored. Rejection by a trusted friend crushes us. However, we are learning that we do have another option for interpreting any experience, and when we seek this new interpretation, we'll not be disturbed any longer.

It's understandable if we don't absorb this principle quickly. It's from a radically different thought system, one that says we never need to see others' mean-spirited actions as anything but their appeals for healing and help. This message is simple. We have heard it many times by now, but it bears repeating: *Only loving thoughts are true; anything else is an appeal for healing and help.*

When we look at our experiences from this perspective, we see all of them quite differently. And we'll respond quite differently too. Disturbing situations dissipate when we shift our perception.

Today will be marvelous if I seek to
experience a marvelous day.

Guidance

 God's voice can be heard above any noise.

Taking time for prayer and meditation is advantageous to everyone. Their importance is lost on no one. Why don't we practice them regularly? The most common excuse is that we are running late and don't have time. Aren't we lucky to have discovered that we needn't take time? We can seek and gain God's wisdom and guidance no matter where we are or what we are doing. We can be in the middle of a conference, a painful confrontation, a job interview, or a tennis game, and God will acknowledge our request for guidance.

Being assured of this is one of the great lessons of life. Too bad it takes so long to learn it, but each time we are saved from a disaster, we sense that a guiding hand was present. We'd profit more if we acknowledged Its presence more often. It's comforting to know that we'll always have the help we need to survive any experience. After all, the situations we encounter are nothing more than our schooling. The best Teacher is only a thought away.

Nothing I do today is unseen by the Holy Spirit.
If I'm having trouble I can ask for help.

The Holy Spirit will solve every problem.

We all know people who seem to attract problems. Job losses follow divorces. Smashed fenders follow confrontations with friends. Perhaps we feel sorry for them. No doubt we're grateful that we don't share their experiences. Why do some people have so much turmoil?

The *Course* teaches that no one has to indefinitely endure painful circumstances. There is one solution to every dilemma: Seek the direction and comfort of the Holy Spirit and problems dissolve. Is it really as simple as it sounds? We may doubt this initially because we can't imagine our acquaintances choosing to experience such turmoil rather than seeking a simple solution. But from the *Course* we also learn about the ego who shares center stage with the Holy Spirit in one's mind. The ego isn't a problem solver in spite of its claim. On the contrary, the ego creates problems.

It's good to know that we all have equal access to the Holy Spirit. It means that none of us is destined to have more problems than others. We can all be as free of problems as we choose to be.

If I have a problem at work or with a family member or even a stranger today, I'll seek the right solution.

August 18

Real World

 This illusory world seems so real.

Everywhere we look, we see evidence that the material plane is real. Perhaps one of the most difficult of all the *Course* ideas to new students is this: *Nothing we see is real.* It's hard to believe because we can touch the fixtures and the people on our path. We exclaim, "How insane to say they're not real!"

The confusion lies in our interpretation of *real.* The *Course* says the real world is simply God, Jesus, the Holy Spirit, and love. That is our home; we are One with it now and always. But in an instant of insanity, we thought we left "home" and we created the ego, who then created the body in which we now reside. Our mission is to remember who we really are and return, in reality, to the place we never really left.

We experience moments of "recall" every day. We might not recognize them as such, but what we feel periodically is the thrill of love, pure love, and Oneness toward whomever we're with. At those moments we have rejoined God and feel exhilarated. We know we want to feel like that again, but we quickly forget the process. We must think only love and we're there.

I am home when I'm in a state of love for all.

Do my thoughts reflect the Spirit or the ego?

How content are we at this moment? *Course* adherents say if we have any agitation, we are in the clutches of the ego. This is a strong statement. Is it always true? The right response is yes, but the ego loves for us to second-guess everything. That's how it maintains control.

Let's accept, then, that agitation means it's time to turn to the Holy Spirit. Does peace come instantly? It can. It's possible to give our thought back to the ego just as quickly, however, putting us back where we were. Fortunately, with enough practice at giving our minds to the Spirit, we'll rest there more frequently. Our lives will change accordingly.

How do I feel today? If I'm not at peace,
I know what to do about it.

August 20

Ego slips
Persistence

 Living the Course *takes practice.*

The ego is enhanced every time we look to it rather than the Holy Spirit for answers or direction. We have formed the habit of turning to the ego first when trouble arises, which means we consciously have to refrain from the habit and just as consciously carve a new one. Thus we say, "Living the *Course* takes practice."

Living the *Course* is a process that only strengthens with use; we have not failed each time we slip and let the ego loose. The *Course* says that slips are okay. There is no time limit because time isn't real. All we have to do is shift our perceptions of a situation from the ego's view to the Holy Spirit's as often as necessary to hone our skill of living the *Course*.

One of the best gifts of this spiritual path is the absence of guilt. That is not to suggest we never have to say we're sorry, but rather, understand that when we listen to the ego instead of the Holy Spirit, transgressions against others result.

I can return to the Holy Spirit's view
as often as needed today.

We can't give our thoughts away.

Our thoughts determine who we are. We may want to push thoughts on others, and no doubt try. But they are still ours. What we can do, however, is change our thoughts. We never have to keep holding a thought we don't want.

Let's say we think a friend has been disparaging us behind our back. We are obsessed with worry and maybe anger. We're afraid of a confrontation, so we keep mulling it over in our minds. How can we get beyond this thought short of approaching our friend? Not surprisingly, the *Course* has a solution: Recognize that thoughts which "attack," whether real or imagined, are a call for love.

Perhaps we aren't willing to offer love or forgiveness when we feel someone has hurt us, but we can decide to give up our own attack thoughts with the help of God. We give them up in the process of changing them, and we change them by asking for a better vision of the situation. A more positive perspective may not come immediately, but that's because the ego still wields control. Be patient and ask again.

*I will look at what I'm thinking today and
make better choices if I'm not happy.*

Relationships

 Relationships can always be seen differently.

We are easily trapped into gauging our value by our security in relationships. We cling to them, making lovers and friends our hostages in the hope of feeling secure and peaceful. What folly! Peace isn't found this way, but the ego says otherwise. That's where the problem lies, of course. We are hostage to the ego just like we make others hostage to us. We all lose in the end.

Whatever spiritual pathway we may have traveled in the past, we always were told our lives had to be right with God. That meant seeing His way. This isn't a difficult concept, but it's easily forgotten. The *Course* reveals that God gave us the Holy Spirit as the "shorthand" to His guidance. Letting the Holy Spirit lead makes us see all people differently. The benefit is that we'll see all relationships differently too.

The security we crave is as close as our shift in perception. Seeing the ego's way or God's is a matter of choice.

*No relationship has to trouble me today. If one is,
I'll ask to see it differently.*

God doesn't create the details of my life.

Most people believe that God knows us intimately. We've probably always liked the idea that God was in charge of every tiny detail of our lives. It meant that we weren't alone and that our lives were unfolding as specified. Coming to believe that God is unaware of "this world" makes us feel extremely vulnerable, abandoned. However, the rest of the "message" is that the Holy Spirit does know us. It guides us, comforts us, assures our peace, offers us a new vision of every circumstance. It was given to us as a gift from God.

We have not been forgotten. We can count on guidance every bit as holy as though it were voiced by God. While it's true that each of us is responsible for the details of our unfolding lives, we don't have to solve any problem alone. In fact, if we dare to try, we'll be relying on the ego and the situation can only become stickier. It's good that we have stuck around this *Course* long enough to get more complete information. Our lives can be much calmer and more joyful now than any set of beliefs made them in the past.

I am not disturbed realizing God isn't in charge of me today.
The Holy Spirit's presence meets my every need.

August 24

Illness

The opportunity to be healed and to heal others is ever present.

Nearly every day we are confronted by evidence of someone's illness. As beginning students of the *Course*, we often resist the idea that people want to have cancer or diabetes or worse. But they do.

Some students walk away from the *Course* rather than try to accept what they don't understand. Those of us sharing these words have chosen the alternative. That doesn't mean we won't struggle against some ideas, but when we do, we can repeatedly ask the Holy Spirit for help in seeing the truth. There is no magic in coming to understand the truth, but there is freedom—freedom from anxiety, guilt, illness, and pain. And when we become free, we are examples that others can emulate.

I will look at the sick today as being well.
How I see myself is how I'll see others.

*The physical world
is a product of the ego.*

For some, this is one of the most difficult of all the *Course* principles. Initially, it even seems frightening. How can we be responsible for the countless tragedies that occur daily around the world? How can earthquakes and famine be products of the ego? Don't they have a reality of their own? Aren't men and women and children really dying?

The best way for us to look at these situations and perhaps understand them within the context of the *Course* is to focus first on small examples of how our minds create our reality. If I expect an argument with a spouse over an issue that concerns us both, it's likely that I'll broach the topic defensively, just waiting for disagreement. Not surprisingly, my action triggers just what I expected. If multitudes of people are fearing and expecting earthquakes and famine, rather than thinking about and creating loving circumstances, the negative energy for devastation may be put in motion.

Thoughts manifest themselves. We can see this in the mundane. With effort we'll be able to glimpse that it may work this way in the extraordinary as well.

*I need to carefully notice what I'm thinking today.
It defines how I see my experiences.*

Guidance

 The Holy Spirit is God's gift to us.

When we feel confused about decisions or afraid because we feel inadequate in some area of our lives, let's remember that we have a helpmate. God didn't abandon us to figure out every detail of our lives. He gave us the next best thing to being here Himself: the Holy Spirit. With the Holy Spirit as close as the next thought, we can always choose the right direction or make the right decision.

Our part of this equation is that we have to seek the guidance that's been promised. How insane that we refrain from doing this, but such is the case. Of course, the ego, which is also as close as the next thought, discourages us from seeking the Holy Spirit's guidance. It bombards us with suggestions that run counter to what the Holy Spirit would tell us. It takes time and many fruitless actions to realize the differences between the two voices. Fortunately, we have all the time we need.

The Holy Spirit is the best gift God could ever have given me.
Today will be full of wonderful surprises if I rely on It.

Conflict or Peace

I will see what I will believe.

That which we see has no inherent reality. Initially, this is startling information, but when we compare our perceptions of events and places with our companions' perceptions, we begin to understand it. It doesn't take many comparisons to realize no two of us see any circumstance alike in every detail. We each see what we want to see to validate the beliefs we're committed to.

If this is human nature, how can we possibly expect people to be free of conflict? In fact, wouldn't this preclude any expectation we may have for peace? Fortunately, there's more to be understood. What the *Course* tells us is that a single action by only one individual can ensure that peace will ultimately reign, even when chaos has struck the group in question.

It's natural that we might doubt this. We see little evidence of truly peaceful gatherings in our communities, but we'll come to understand this principle best by taking the single action the *Course* suggests. And what is it? It's asking the Holy Spirit for a perspective other than the one of conflict. It will come and so will peace.

I am responsible for what I see today. Looking through the eyes of the Holy Spirit will offer me a peaceful picture.

Fear

We have a lifeline to God.

Nearly every day something happens that triggers fear in us. People criticize us, family members don't answer our calls, job interviews get canceled. We shudder with fear trying to manage the everyday uncertainties. If only we'd remember that we have access to the perfect manager for every situation.

Our experiences here, in this illusory world, have been requested by us. That doesn't mean we'll know how to handle any of them. It simply means that what we need to learn, while in these bodies, is contained within the situations that beckon. We'll assimilate them far more successfully if we seek the company of the Holy Spirit while we explore and absorb them. Nothing that comes to us can really harm us if we see it through the eyes of God, and this perspective is always with us.

If we're filled with fear or anger at any time, we need to tug on our lifeline. God can't help us, ever, if we don't initiate His involvement.

*I will have peace today if I seek the involvement
of the Holy Spirit.*

Our fear of love attracts the ego.

It seems contradictory that we fear love, particularly in light of how skillfully we create special relationships in our attempts to receive love. In reality, we make hostages of our lovers to prevent the rejection we think we deserve.

The ego has a heyday when we enter into relationships. It never loves our partners unconditionally. It never really loves at all, in fact. Through control and guilt, it works overtime trying to prevent our companions from having a life of their own. Such would mean we'd been rejected, not loved, and that's our worst fear.

How can we break this unhealthy pattern of living? Before studying the *Course,* we no doubt thought we couldn't. And even now we backslide often. But we are learning some simple tools. We can't feel or offer love except with the Holy Spirit's help. Letting the ego say or decide anything for us will never result in our knowing love.

The ego is waiting to pounce on everybody today.
Loving and being loved is another option I can choose.

Right Mind

 What world am I grounded in?

The idea that there is more than one world mystifies us when we first come to *A Course in Miracles.*® Isn't what we see real? The answer is, not necessarily. The longer we practice the *Course* ideas, however, the happier we are to discover how easily we can journey from the world we see to the one we'd rather see. This journey is frequently necessary because we wander away from the safety of the Holy Spirit's world too easily.

The level of our joy and peacefulness instantly reveals where our journey has taken us each moment of the day. If we are anxious and uncertain about anything in our lives, we have journeyed to the ego's stomping grounds. Nothing says we can't stay there for a while. We're free to wander wherever we choose. But if we want to know love, if we want to experience peace, we have taken a wrong turn. We'll never experience peace through the ego.

I can be wherever I want to be today.
Does joy beckon?

August 31

*Forgiveness in this world is
equivalent to love in Heaven.*

Why is it so hard to forgive others' character defects? Not only do we resist forgiving them, we contemplate aggressive punishment in many cases. We have been told by other *Course* students that, in reality, we cower from forgiving ourselves. And when we can finally forgive ourselves, we discover that our resentments toward others have dissipated.

Why are we so hard on ourselves, and consequently, others? It's owing to the guilt we feel for having "exchanged" God's world for this painful and silly charade. In one insane moment we refused God's unconditional love, and this nightmare is the result.

We don't relish remaining here because the anxiety is so great. But the ego puts up a struggle every time we choose to honor God's memory. Fortunately, God placed the Holy Spirit in our minds when we "escaped." That's our ticket back. In time, we will make the final journey home.

*I am on a mission today to return to my real home.
I will contemplate the memory of God that's within me.*

SEPTEMBER

Miracles are available to everyone.

We have all experienced people who seem to have a miraculous gift for spreading good will. Circumstances are positively enhanced and problems get smoothly resolved when they are present. We may envy them, not realizing we *share* their gift.

How we think—the way we perceive a situation—is always open to interpretation. Bringing the love and peace of the Holy Spirit to any experience will give us a far different perspective than seeing it from the ego's point of view. The ego creates no miracles. It's bent on destruction, in fact.

It doesn't take but an instant to make a miracle. Changing our minds is all that's necessary. The hard part is remembering that the ego has us in its clutches every minute that we aren't holding the hand of God. Taking God's hand lifts us from the turmoil the ego has created.

*My experiences today can be as miraculous as my
little willingness to take the hand of God.*

September 2

Perspective

 The purpose of the Course *is to see differently.*

How many of us are as happy as we'd hoped to be? Most of us had expectations of relationships, jobs, homes, and children that have not developed as anticipated. But have the results been wrong or bad? Haven't they simply been different from what we'd imagined?

Seeing what has occurred from even a slightly different perspective is refreshing. Let's assume, for instance, that we do have exactly the job that's meant for us. And further, let's believe that the relationship we're in is quite specifically the one for us, that both this job and this partner are the avenues mandatory for the lessons we need.

How differently we feel about our circumstances when we change, even slightly, how we think about them. The opportunity to change how we see anything is always a possibility now that we've learned how.

All I have to do in order to get a different picture is ask.
Today can be peaceful. It's up to me.

Conflict

Peace can never coexist with conflict.

Do we gain anything in our many conflicts with others? We may think we do, particularly if we gain esteem from influencing others' opinions. But the pathway to that point of general agreement is often tension-filled and uncertain. There's no peace to be felt in those circumstances.

We have to decide if being peaceful appeals to us more than being right. For some, gratifying the ego takes precedence. Those people will live in perpetual conflict, perhaps never knowing that life could be experienced another way. That's their prerogative, of course. Unfortunately, because it's necessary for us to interact with myriad personalities, we'll frequently be faced with the decision to fight or take flight.

Seeing all interactions as our opportunities for moments of peacefulness lessens our dread. The decision to walk away is quite empowering. We may even begin to look for these opportunities.

Today I will focus on the benefits of creating peace.

Right Mind

*No thought of fear can enter a mind
while it thinks of God.*

None of us has escaped being afraid. Some of us have been afraid most of our lives. We've tried many remedies. Alcohol and drugs may have beckoned as escapes from fear. The reprieve was short-lived, however. Meditation, visualization, and nervous prayer may also have appealed to us, leading to a modicum of success. Workaholism, illness, and an overcommitted social life have been tried by some as solutions. None of these worked for long, but there is one solution that is guaranteed. Thank goodness it's been introduced to us at last.

The solution we all have access to, in an instant, is bringing to our minds the thought of God. Sound simple? It is. It is also effective. When our minds are filled with thoughts of God, they cannot hold any other thought. Neither fear nor anger nor confusion can hinder one who dwells on God.

Does this mean we must think of nothing else? Obviously, shopping, working, and household responsibilities might carry our thoughts away. But we can return them to God when even the tiniest problem arises. What a solution!

☯

I will be unafraid today, totally unafraid.

There must be another way.

It's said that Helen Schucman's colleague, Bill Thetford, made this simple statement to Helen just before Jesus began dictating His message to her: There must be another way. Thousands of lives have dramatically and positively changed because of the message. Millions more are destined to. How exciting that we're part of that lucky group.

It almost seems too simple that such an ordinary statement could trigger major changes in how people think, thus experience their lives. But, indeed, that's what has happened. When we make the decision to seek *another way* to see or solve a problem, we have opened the door to the Holy Spirit. Absolutely no situation looks or feels the same when the Holy Spirit has been consulted.

It's a relief to know that our lives can be as simple as we choose to make them. We don't have to struggle with anyone about anything. We don't have to worry over any situation. Whatever level of peace we desire is available, on demand.

Q

*Today I will remember that there is always another
way to proceed if I'm stuck.*

September 6

Truth

 Only loving thoughts are true.

The *Course* clearly delineates between the truth and everything else. Using this principle to measure all actions clarifies and interprets all the circumstances that involve us. Our response to any situation or person need never vary. Attack is never appropriate regardless of how the experience has manifested.

It's not easy to accept that the mean-spirited actions of others are their calls for healing and help. And the ego quickly justifies our own mean reactions. Let's not judge ourselves negatively for that. Instead, let's be aware of our negative thoughts and actions. Then we need to ask to feel another way about the individual who has triggered the feeling. Forgiveness will always be possible if we ask for it.

There is a simpler way to live than most of us enjoy. It results from our willingness to let the Holy Spirit decide all actions, think all thoughts, make all plans. We'll never need to seek healing and help if we live in this manner.

*Can I hold only loving thoughts today? There is
a way and it's open to me.*

As one is healed, all are healed.

Perhaps it doesn't appear as though we are One, but in the world of God, Oneness is all there is. When we observe our separate minds and separate diseased bodies, we aren't seeing the Real World. The miracle of healed minds exists only in the Real World.

Our task is to think only love, to feel only forgiveness if we hope to attain the freedom from illness that we deserve. But sometimes we seek, instead, to hold a grudge or to elicit pity. We can't expect to be well when that's the case. It's only because we forgot the parameters of the holy relationship that we sought to get our way through the shadow of illness. Such folly hinders most of us on occasion, but nothing is forever without our acquiescence.

Deciding to be well is deciding to let the Holy Spirit do our *deciding* for us.

I can contribute to the health of all my friends today
by taking care to do right by my own health.

Lessons

What can I learn from this situation?

Everything that happens to us can be spiritually enlightening. Trusting this principle can lessen the trauma of any situation. The loss of a loved one hurts, but we remember that God never leaves us. The disappearance of a favorite possession may upset us, but we know possessions don't love us and we can survive without them.

We're moving along a learning curve, passing other students one day and being passed the next. Our destination is the same; we're going home to rejoin God and forget this tiny, mad nightmare we have been living.

We find great relief in remembering that no experience is so big or so awful we can't quickly decipher the lesson and move on. Not getting bogged down in trivia refreshes us.

Today's lessons have my name on them.

Let's dispense with all battles.

The world we inhabit would look entirely different if there were no more battles. It sounds like an impossible dream, doesn't it? But it could transpire were we all to join with the Holy Spirit, thus one another, at the same moment in time. Until then, each of us can make a small, but meaningful, contribution toward the goal every time we express a loving thought to another human being.

Some of us have personalities that are easily agitated. For us, the loving thoughts seem few and not very genuine, perhaps. It's important to understand that we're responsible for cultivating the kind of personalities we have every minute we're present in this world. If we want to be like someone else, that's always an option. We simply have to act and think accordingly.

If fighting is our thing, we can trigger it by attracting other ego-intense people to share our journey. But if we tire of the tension, a different way to live is readily available. Might we try it on for size?

I can have as many battles as my companions are willing to recognize today. Or I can be at peace.

Responsibility

Every thought we hold manifests somewhere.

Consider this: If we choose to think of a co-worker as detrimental to our success at work, we'll respond to him in a suspicious, attacking manner. He'll likely respond in kind. We'll have created a situation that mirrors our perception. Every thought we hold manifests somewhere. This extremely powerful idea is both frightening and exhilarating.

If the principle works this successfully for negative thinking, can we expect it to work similarly when we hold only love in our minds? That's the good news. Whatever we hold in our minds, whichever *voice* forms our thoughts, determines how we see our companions and how we experience our lives minute by minute. In other words, if we are having a bad day, we are having "bad" thoughts. The decision to change our minds, thus our thoughts, can be made as often as necessary.

I will be accountable for how my day is going.
If I don't like how it feels, it's up to me to
monitor my thoughts and change them.

What God creates is real. Nothing more.

We have arrived at this point in our spiritual development from many schools of thought. Some of us were raised to believe that God watched over every move we made, noting each one in a black book. We'd have to account for ourselves one day and we'd be properly punished. Others believed in a loving God but still assumed that every happening in one's life was dictated by God for our own good. Our tragedies were explained as God's tests designed to strengthen our faith.

The beliefs we're introduced to in the *Course* are radically different from these, which makes it hard for many of us initially. We're not comfortable discarding everything our parents or ministers or other trusted friends told us. And we don't have to do this immediately. Taking in new ideas one at a time is quite enough. Beginning with "What God creates is real" deserves lots of pondering. The *Course* says that what He creates never changes. Most of what we see in the illusory world does change. That can only mean God wasn't the Creator. Let's meditate upon this for as long as needed. Understanding will come.

Today I will be willing to understand what I
need to about the Real World.

Illusory world

We need help to escape from this illusory world.

This experience we're having seems so real, doesn't it? It's difficult to grasp that our perceptions have created whatever we're seeing. If we change our perceptions, we'll change the experience. But how do we change our perceptions? They seem to just happen.

On the contrary, they don't simply happen. The ego vies for control of our perceptions, and when what we see triggers anger or fear, we know the ego is painting the picture. At these moments, were we to go back to the drawing board to seek another picture, one drawn by the Holy Spirit, we'd have a far different experience.

What we see and feel and think is always up to us. If we don't like what's going on around us, we can leave that scene behind. It's a small decision that can be made and remade at will. Let's practice.

My perception will change at will.
Today is an open book.

What's an appeal for healing and help?

We easily recognize anger or fear or distress in another person. But many of us never considered those characteristics as cries for help. It's far more likely that we judged them and then reacted to them as examples of arrogance or inferiority. Our response defined us well.

Just because we don't perceive another's action as an appeal for healing and help doesn't mean we can't learn to see it that way with a little willingness. The principle we must come to cherish fully is that *any loving thought is true; anything else is a cry for healing and help.* This allows for an easy distinction whenever we're observing another's actions. This doesn't mean we won't judge someone or even condemn them. However, the first step in changing ourselves, if that's what we want to do, is changing our attitude about what we see outside of ourselves. The next step is vigilance. That's beyond none of us.

If someone is behaving badly today, I can be willing to recognize what they are asking for.

Relationships

 Destructive relationships can be transformed.

Friends generally recommend that we get out of destructive relationships. That may be good advice. However, there is another idea to consider. We might choose to redefine the relationship, but it takes our genuine willingness to change how we perceive the relationship now. And if it's physically or mentally destructive, we may not choose to do that. Indeed, perhaps we shouldn't.

The important idea here is that we can create a shift in our perception of a relationship. We can't do it alone, and we can't do it with the ego's help. We can do it, however, if we invite the Holy Spirit into the relationship. It helps when both people want the Holy Spirit's involvement, but even if only one requests it, a change in how he or she perceives the relationship will occur.

One might still choose to leave it, but the reasons for doing so will be different. It won't be done in anger or fear. It will happen because it should happen; the guidance was offered and accepted. The destruction has ended and this relationship has been transformed.

My relationships can be changed today. If I want one to be different, I simply need to seek help from the Holy Spirit.

Let's seek to understand our Oneness.

Perhaps the most elusive of all the *Course* ideas is that we are One; we are not separate in any way. Everything we look at in this world of experiences suggests the opposite to us. It takes a Herculean suspension of our disbelief to see beyond our physical differences. We have forgotten, so successfully, the memory of our wholeness with God and each other that we must constantly seek the Holy Spirit's help to remember this truth.

Probably every conflict, every moment of our discontent is related to our dealings with another person. What beautiful irony. Only when we come to understand that we are in a dream here, not in the Real World where all is One, do we begin to see how insane our perceptions, and thus conflicts, are.

How do we capture the memory of our Oneness, which is so well hidden in our minds? There is only one way. It's by the decision to believe that this is so and then the willingness to ask the only one who can show us this truth for evidence. The Holy Spirit will always respond to our request.

☉

I really don't need conflict in my life today. If I seek to see my brothers and sisters as myself, I can relinquish the urge to argue.

Special relationships

 Special relationships are not really special.

Most of us are quite surprised to learn that "special" doesn't mean what we'd always thought it meant. Before embarking on this journey, we had labeled our most significant relationships as special. Now we're told that special relationships aren't loving ones at all. Rather, they're a coming together of individuals who covertly seek to control each other for personal gain and security. The parameters in these "friendships" are forever shifting and no one is ever secure or at peace.

It's not hard to recognize how special we've made many of our relationships. The struggle to control someone is all consuming. Realistically, it always fails too, but we're not eager to acknowledge this. We've based so much of our own identity on what we succeed in getting from someone else that we resist giving up our attempts. Who would we be if we were not opposing someone? That's what we're here to learn. The Holy Spirit is always ready to show us a different kind of relationship. When we're ready, the opportunity will arise.

My relationships can reflect either struggle or peace.
Today I'll choose peace.

This world is a training ground, nothing more.

Interpreting our daily experiences as a kind of training changes them significantly. Daily occurrences have neither the profound importance nor the long-term, sustained impact that we'd assumed. They serve to move us along in our journey, nothing more. And where is our journey taking us? We're headed toward the Real World, the home we abandoned so long ago.

Our reason for leaving "home" isn't terribly important. In an instant, we left, and our lives have been chaotic ever since. Fortunately, the door is always open for our return, and even though we may not be ready to stay permanently, we get a chance to experience the peace that awaits us there each time we contemplate the comfort and presence of God.

It's a relief to learn that no event is particularly important all by itself. Its role is to educate us, not shame or intimidate us. Let's take a fresh look at our experiences and enjoy them for their real purpose, then let them go.

*Every experience is an opportunity to learn. I'll remember this
today and not be fearful of any situation.*

Judging others

*We can't hear God's voice
when we're judging someone.*

We don't always want to hear God's voice. There are moments when we love the power we feel while judging others. The high is short-lived, however. Inevitably we experience guilt commensurate with our judgments.

Fortunately, God's voice of love and forgiveness quietly waits for our willingness to hear it. We'll not see our experiences or our companions in the same way when we listen to God's message regarding them. Why would we ever choose to turn away?

The answer lies in the insanity of the ego. If we're not extremely cautious in our focus, it will grab our attention and command our reactions. We can think only attack when the ego is in charge. One or the other voice will always be heard. Which do we want it to be?

*Today I will remember that judging others jeopardizes
my sense of peace.*

Problems

Peace is found only in God.

Probably the most common feeling we experience in *this world* is doubt. We're not sure what to do in many situations, so we become afraid, sometimes to the point of paralysis. We seek resolution for our perceived problems from people who are frequently as uncertain as us. Anxiety results and it's often followed by misdirected anger. Our frustration occasionally seems unending. Fortunately, that's never really the case. We're just beginning to learn that our experiences can be profoundly different.

What do we actually seek? Quite likely it's much the same for all of us. We want to trust that we'll be okay in all situations, and we want to feel the joy that accompanies real peace. This doesn't have to elude us any longer. It's as available as our desire for it. We simply have to dismiss the thoughts we so often harbor and insist instead for the memory of God to come to our mind. It's not a mysterious request. Most of us simply haven't taken enough advantage of it. The better habit we form, the more sustained will be our peacefulness.

I can be peace-filled and joyful today if I seek the comfort of God in all matters.

September 20

Call for help

 Someone's call for help is our invitation for union.

No two calls for help will look alike. Each appeal will mirror the ego voicing it. Some will be subtle, quietly manipulative, but destructive nonetheless. Others will be easily identified and reviled because of their intensity and mean-spiritedness. We'll not wish to forgive some calls. Others we'll not even recognize.

Why should we concern ourselves with another's appeal for help and healing, particularly if it's not easily recognized? There's only one reason. Answering the call with forgiveness, thus love, is the pathway back to our real home. We made the decision to come *here,* or rather the ego did, but our intention is not to stay. The occasional glimmers of recall we have of the Real World, of Heaven, invite our return. We note them but often don't remember them. Each time another appeal is made, we hear the invitation again.

Joining with others happens when we forgive them for their actions, be they overt or quiet. The barriers we construct between us seem to melt away. Our Oneness is then apparent.

My joining with another soul today heals us both.
I will look forgivingly on my brothers and sisters.

Separation

*We can live in our body without any thought
of separation or attack.*

We aren't separate from God. It's a totally mad idea to think we are. That's what the ego tries to make us think, however, as its way of controlling our lives. If we could know our Oneness with God at all times, we'd never end up in chaotic messes.

The idea that we are really One with God and other people is good news. It's also a bit mysterious. Our eyes see where our bodies end and other bodies begin. How can we all be *One in God?*

Let's suspend our disbelief. Accepting that we are all part of God must be taken on faith. God gave us the Holy Spirit in our minds to act as the reminder, the bridge to our real identity. Remembering its presence gives us the willingness to relinquish all thought of attack on another. After all, there is no other. There is only God as all of us.

*Today I will remember that attacking others attacks God.
The Holy Spirit will help me see the Real World.*

September 22

Healing

 We are responsible for how this day unfolds.

The society we live in is our creation. God didn't make war or famine or disease. We often hear others say when faced with a catastrophe, "God is surely testing me." But no principle of the *Course* supports this idea. On the contrary, it says God created no part of this illusory world at all! This is radically different from the belief system with which most of us grew up. The tendency to discard this new system is overwhelming on occasion. The ego likes it that way.

What does this mean in practical terms? It means that unless we invite the Holy Spirit to speak through us in every encounter, we'll continue adding to the destruction around us. Every time we create a positive shift in our perceptions of an event, we are contributing to the betterment of us all. How we see either heals or destroys. Taking control away from the ego is our daily assignment and the Holy Spirit is our willing tutor.

Today I will reject the insanity of the ego and seek only peace.

Whatever is true *and* real *will never die.*

It is so easy to forget that what we look upon is not real. We can touch that which we see and formulate thoughts and feelings about it. Therefore, it greatly challenges our minds to accept that nothing we see here in the illusory world is real.

Our process for full acceptance of this idea can be helped by our willingness to note the instability, the change in form, the eventual death of every living entity we observe. This realization, coupled with the *Course* principle that what is real is forever changeless, formless, and eternal, offers us a different perspective.

What's the value of truly understanding this principle? It allows us to look beyond and through the people we see to the Spirit within them. It removes our need to judge or react to that which we have created. We can be peaceful rather than agitated when we see the eternal Spirit present everywhere.

My observations of everyone and everything will match
my decision about what to see today.

September 24

Angst

*We feel angst because
this world isn't our real home.*

We long to be home. The only peace we'll ever know awaits us there. Why are we here? How did we get here and why do we stay? It's some consolation to learn that we're only *here* as temporary students. That implies that we'll eventually "graduate." But what then? Will our lives really be different?

What we're told is that our home, the Real World, knows only peace and love. There is no turmoil, no strife of any kind there. What we are only finally glimpsing though, is that we don't have to leave these bodies and these experiences to be there. We merely have to choose another vision of these experiences. It's not complicated, but the paranoid ego keeps us trapped.

We can free ourselves from the ego at any time. Why not now? Our angst will be gone immediately.

*My choice is to feel joy or pain today.
No one chooses for me.
What do I really want?*

Let's not let our minds wander.

A wandering mind can't be a dangerous thing, can it? Isn't a wandering mind a relaxed mind, a peaceful one? The answer is occasionally yes; however, if we let our minds wander unattended too often, they get snatched up by the ego and then we're in trouble. When the ego grabs hold of our minds, we see culprits who aren't really there, we feel fear that has no basis, we plan attacks on others that will harm all of us.

Must we be vigilant every moment regarding the workings of the mind? Yes, but it's not as difficult as it may sound to keep the mind in check. It's primarily a decision, and we instantly know when we have wandered off from the Holy Spirit because we start feeling fear. Fear is ever present when the mind wanders too far from God and love and the belief that we have purpose in this physical realm.

We aren't perfect. That's why we're still on this journey. Dropping the hand of God is an everyday occurrence for some of us. All of us remember the peacefulness of holding God's hand. We will reach for it again. Always.

*I will monitor my thinking today. I'll know instantly when
I have dropped the hand of the God.*

Right Mind

We have no private thoughts.
All thoughts are shared.

Simply realizing that every one of our thoughts impacts others, either quietly or quite noticeably, motivates us to monitor what we are thinking. No thought is meaningless, because we affect others with our attitudes.

Let's take care to invite the Holy Spirit to help us form our thoughts. They will be decidedly different from the ones the ego creates. The Holy Spirit will not make us compare ourselves with others. Nor will it think mean-spirited thoughts or foist ill wishes on any person. The Holy Spirit thinks only love. When the Holy Spirit is in charge, we nurture the people around us. Everyone is affected by the love we formulate in our minds. The nasty thoughts are just as powerful.

I will think only love today.
The people around me will benefit.
So will I.

Perspective

Nothing has to change.

So many times a day we lament a particular situation, certain that our lives could be vastly improved if only it changed. And when that doesn't seem possible, we focus on the people involved, in hopes that they will change. Can it be true that nothing has to change in order for our experience to be different? Indeed, that's the case. But how?

When the particulars of a situation stay the same, it's natural for us to assume that our reaction and the outcome will be the same too. That's what past experience has taught us. But we are learning something different now, and it's vastly important. It can change every experience we'll ever have; consequently, our lives will unfold in a way that's unimaginable to us now.

We are learning that we can see any experience in a wholly unexpected way simply by seeking another perspective. Not a single aspect has to change for us to see it differently. That's miraculous! Our lives will never be the same.

I can handle whatever is happening today.
How I see it is in my control.

Violence

Are we willing to give up attack thoughts?

The signs of human aggression are everywhere. Newspapers recount them; television reports them; magazines and movies often exaggerate and glorify them. It's difficult to imagine a nonaggressive world. We may wonder what good it would do if we gave up our aggression, our desires to attack others. In a world such as this one, wouldn't we be taken advantage of?

The point of giving up attack thoughts, according to the *Course,* is for the reward that's guaranteed. We'll discover a peacefulness we had never known when we relinquish our attack thoughts. We'll realize that others seek only love in the guise of their attacks. We have to decide if we want peace, of course, and if we haven't experienced it very often, we may not appreciate its value.

Let's experiment with this idea. Whenever we get the desire to attack someone today, replace the thought with the idea of God. Replace the feeling with an offering of love. That's all we ever really want. That's all others really want too.

I can give up all attack thoughts for this one day.
How will it feel?

God knows no wrath.

Regardless of our religious "education," most of us have heard that God punishes us for our "sins." What we assumed our sins were depended partly on who our parents were. Some of us grew up "guiltier" than others. But no doubt all of us grew up believing that God watched every move and waited to get us.

As adults, we know that's not really true. But do we actually believe, as the *Course* dictates, that God is in Heaven, not here at all, thus not even aware of our good or bad deeds? That's a radical departure from what most of us were taught. If God isn't involved in our lives now, what does it matter how we behave?

Even though God is not *here,* we are not abandoned. The Holy Spirit accompanies us on this journey and guides us as God would guide us. We'll only receive love from the Holy Spirit. We'll be guided to offer only love to others too. We'll never be punished, no matter what we do. It's never our job to punish others either.

The only wrath I'll ever feel is what the ego metes out.
The Holy Spirit will only love me today.

Love

Love cannot attack.

We mistakenly claim to be loving people. While it may be true that we regularly express signs of affection toward children or parents and friends, we sometimes respond hatefully to individuals in our daily experiences. We can't be both hateful and loving. If we withhold love and affirmation from one, we are, in essence, withholding them from everyone. It's a simple principle and it holds true in every instance.

Let's not dismiss ourselves as wholly unworthy just because we aren't perfect examples of love. We do have another option. We can decide to think more about love and we can monitor more carefully how we treat all people. When we are inclined toward an unloving action or thought, let's ask the Holy Spirit for a different one. While it's true that we have to want to do our part, it's also true that we'll always get what we ask for.

Q

Before I make a move today,
I'll decide who I want to be.

OCTOBER

Allowing the Holy Spirit to extend love
through us is a miracle.

In the past we may have thought of miracles as physical events: the saved life, the cured disease, the unexpected birth. These occurrences, however, aren't the only examples of miracles. We feel miracles; they don't depend on physical proof. In other words, miracles exist in our minds. What better place for them? It means we can all personally experience miracles daily.

Allowing our minds to express joy, happiness, and serenity means offering love as a matter of course. To do this, we need to align with the Holy Spirit rather than the ego, but that's no challenge. It's a decision we can make at will. Until we have a history of doing this, we can't anticipate how smoothly our day will flow. That's the miracle!

Being a "miracle-maker" is work we all have been called to do. No matter what profession or job we may have prepared for, it pales in comparison to the benefits of extending the love of the Holy Spirit to one another.

I will do my part in creating a miracle today.

October 2

Retribution

God does not condemn.

It's startling information that God is not a part of *this world*. We were probably taught that God not only watched us and protected us, but also held us accountable for our transgressions. The condemnation we received for those "sins," often at the hands of ministers or punishing parents, was to *appease* God.

The *Course* insists that God doesn't punish, that we are never less than perfect in God's world. Because our behavior belies this often, what are we to believe? Acceptance doesn't come easy, but we're told to believe that what we see and think and do *here* aren't real, aren't true, at least not according to God. Does this mean we can freely attack others? Not exactly. We can, of course, if we must, but the text teaches that whatever we do to another, we are doing to ourselves. Its simple suggestion is that we seek an alternative behavior. An idea for one will come.

Today I will remember that God never punishes me.

Who needs forgiveness today?

We sometimes find ourselves surrounded by friends and colleagues who irritate us. It's normal to gravitate toward men and women who frequently incite our anger. There's an explanation for this. The *Course* teaches that everything we observe and feel about others is a direct projection of our own shortcomings. This is not an easy principle to accept, particularly when there is so much in others that engenders our irritation. It helps to learn that our sole purpose *here* is to *know* forgiveness. It's evident, pretty quickly, that we need to forgive ourselves.

If we weren't so disgusted with ourselves, we'd not be so eager to bring others down too. The obvious first task is to be more tolerant of our own failings, acknowledging that to be human is to be imperfect. Next, we must forgive ourselves. This isn't easy, but with the help of the Holy Spirit, we can come to believe that we deserve love. After developing compassion for ourselves, we'll be able to feel it for others. It doesn't just happen; we have to work at it. But a transformation is guaranteed and eventually everyone "looks" okay.

I will be surrounded by folks who deserve forgiveness today.
Who I see is who I am!

Confusion
Real World

God is changeless and eternal.

Whenever we feel confused regarding this material world versus the Real World, we need only note the nearest tree or flower or person. Change is forever visible. Death is the ultimate reality *here.* The same is not true in the world made by God, the world we left, the world we'll return to someday. But for now, we're here, and when our lessons have been learned, we'll receive the gift of the eternal once again.

What's so good about the changeless, eternal world? Would we really prefer it? We are assured we would by our Teachers and the *Course* writings. Perhaps it's hard to imagine a life with no strife, but that's what awaits us. The peace we'd feel is an ecstasy unimaginable here. Fortunately, we can get glimpses of this peace whenever we express only love. Time stands still and all remains changeless in those moments of pure loving. That quiet change-lessness is peace and wholeness and Oneness with God.

If all around me I see confusion and fear,
I'll retreat to the peace within.
My home is with God today,
if I so choose.

Our split minds are our way home.

Admitting to a "split mind" seems unsound. But if we consider how dramatically different we feel on some occasions than others, maybe we'll understand this concept better. We have all experienced moments of rage, times when we desperately wanted to hurt someone, and we have felt utter, total compassion for a friend in pain, perhaps in the same hour. How can the same mind embody such opposite feelings?

Learning that our minds are split, that they have two parts, explains the opposing views. We soon realize that we can rely on one part or the other for our response to any situation that presents itself. Which one we choose makes all the difference in how a situation unfolds.

When we seek the ego's advice to a situation, we'll generally fantasize an attack. If the Holy Spirit's wisdom is sought, we'll feel the love of God and be overcome with peacefulness. With practice, we'll come to prefer the latter.

I will call on the Holy Spirit and experience peace today.

Holy Spirit

The Holy Spirit protects us.

If we really understood who the Holy Spirit is and even more important, how accessible It is, we'd sail through our experiences unruffled. Where are we going wrong?

In our madness to escape God and the Real World, we forgot who we really are. God, as the Creator, didn't forget us, however, and placed the Holy Spirit in us as our perpetual companion to safeguard us, to comfort us, to answer all our questions. We will never be at a loss for the right decision or the best response to a situation or a person. Through the Holy Spirit, God continues to guide every move we make, providing we seek the guidance. It doesn't come unbidden.

Are we still confused? Let's think of this Spirit as a guardian angel whose wings brush away the fear and turmoil of our lives. Of course, we can give It any form we want, whatever seems most appropriate to us. The important element is simply the decision to turn to the Holy Spirit for whatever help we need.

Today will unfold according to the dictates of the Holy Spirit
if I choose to ask It for help.

What we perceive we have projected.

How can we be held responsible for all the troubling, perhaps even dangerous, circumstances we encounter?

Even though we may not easily understand that what we perceive we have projected, we can successfully change the experiences we have by changing how we perceive them. The change has to start with us, not with others. Within our minds, we "author" our lives. However they unfold, we must be held accountable.

How can we best use this power? We no doubt have a history of bad experiences because of how we misused the power. That doesn't have to be the picture of the future though. What we "see" is decided by who we put in charge of "seeing." If we designate the ego as our lookout, we'll often be on the receiving end of anger and attack. Let's choose again. The Holy Spirit is always in the wings.

I will see joy today if I really want it.

Guidance

 We can change our minds, nothing more.

Nothing can disturb us if we realize we only need to change our minds about it. No person can get under our skin, no situation can haunt or frighten us, no longer would the anticipation of a future event hold us hostage. The freedom suggested here isn't imaginary. It's the very miracle that adopting the *Course* principles guarantees.

We have all spent countless years trying to change other people and the circumstances in our lives. We've done this because of our own fears of not fitting in. If only someone or something else were different, we'd be safe, we thought. Our fears only grew. The number of situations that we tried to control unsuccessfully only multiplied. At long last we have discovered a new approach to living.

How do we change our minds? We ask this tiny question of the Holy Spirit: "Will you help me see what's happening now in another way?" Our minds will change instantly. We may have to repeat the request, many times at first, but we will get results.

I can have a different vision of everything I see today if the one I've made up doesn't bring me peace.

Choice
Real World

This is a terrible world.

If we believe, as the *Course* teaches, that this world is a nightmare the ego made, we can agree that it's terrible. The violence, death, and destruction are too insane to be God's creations. But what purpose are they serving? Why did we come and what's our role here?

These are lofty questions we're confronting; however, we don't need answers. Our companions on this journey help us see that we have the world we deserve. When we see through the eyes of the ego we won't want what we receive. We'll come to understand we'll get what we want when we look through different eyes.

The Real World is not the one we often see, but it's always available to us. The more committed we are to changing how we see the circumstances in our lives, the more often we'll see and contribute to the peaceful Real World.

The world I see is up to me.
Today can be a fresh start.

Ego

Do we really believe God is cruel?

If we believe God created this world, we'd have to hold Him accountable for war, child molestation, mass murder, earthquakes, insanity, poverty. We'd have to assume He is exceedingly cruel if we assume anything at all. That isn't a comforting idea. In fact, it's frightening. What will He do next if He's responsible for all this heartache?

A Course in Miracles® says God doesn't cause any disturbance. But if He didn't, who did? The *Course's* answer is not comforting because it places responsibility wholly on us. We can't imagine why we'd ever want to wreak havoc on an unsuspecting world.

Perhaps we'll never understand it, but let's accept that we have a deluded ego that's holding us and everyone else hostage for as long as we listen to it. Taking the chance to not listen allows us to hear the truth about ourselves, our companions, our world.

If the world I see today looks mean and bleak,
I am letting the ego be my eyes.

Real World

The memory of our "home" never left us.

Not all memories give us pleasure, and we sometimes dwell on those that injured our bodies or our spirits. It's never beneficial to dredge up the painful past because it distorts the present. A good habit to form is whenever we think about yesterday or before, give the moment, instead, to thoughts of God. We'll feel instantly healed of the past trauma if we refuse to let its memory linger.

There is one memory that never hurts us. That's the memory of the Real World, a place of love, peace, and joy presided over by God. Fortunately, we can't forget this memory, not for long anyway. The ego tries to damage it, but our ties to God's world, through the Holy Spirit in our minds, can't be severed completely. Knowing that the Holy Spirit is always there waiting for our safe return softens the blows we encounter in this world.

I will remember "home" today if trouble begins to brew.

Guidance
Responsibility

Who is responsible for this world?

Don't we all want to blame somebody else for even the smallest of our troubles? The lost billfold, the forgotten appointment, the spoiled dinner surely can't be solely our fault. We never intended those things to happen.

Perhaps we would not resist being accountable if we didn't take the mistakes so much to heart. In this, the *Course* can be a great help, allowing us to see that our experiences are simply tools for learning the lessons we are ready for. It's what our minds do with the lessons that's significant. The ego wants us to feel guilty for any *imperfect* action. Guilt makes us ashamed and it multiplies.

Fortunately we are learning that even the most irresponsible actions don't have to shadow us for long if we ask the Holy Spirit for guidance. It doesn't take the burden of responsibility off of us, but it lets the experience serve a useful purpose.

I am responsible for my life today.
God will help me live it well.

Anger

Anger is an appeal for healing and help.

It's ironic that someone who longs for love lashes out at friends and strangers alike. What can they possibly be thinking? Their actions push others away. The sad truth is that angry people are consumed with fear about even the tiny details of life. Because of their fear, they intimidate others, thus the love they crave isn't available to them.

The teachings of the *Course* help us recognize how fear may be motivating a friend or family member. How fortunate for them that we can choose forgiveness and love, rather than retaliation, as our response. Offering unconditional love to everyone is always the appropriate response. With friends and lovers, it's not a difficult choice. When mean-spirited co-workers or nasty neighbors strike out at us, it's not easy to look beyond their anger. But when we make the effort, we realize the lack of love they feel. That's our cue to acknowledge their appeal appropriately.

It's not easy to look beyond the meanness of others, but I will make every effort to help another person heal today.

Who is making our decisions?

Nothing external to us has any meaning except what we bring to it. Therefore, if a problem arises, we have to look solely at ourselves. The advantage is we need look only to ourselves if we want to change our lives. Playing the waiting game, as many of us have done—waiting for people to change, waiting for circumstances to change, waiting for expectations to change—need not detain us any longer. If we want anything to be different, let's get moving!

Making changes is not complicated, unless it's another person we want to change. That's an impossibility. However, we will discover how changed they will seem when we make a change in ourselves. Whatever we see in others depends on how we look at them, and which *inner eye* we look through. This principle is set.

Who we put in charge of how we see today will determine everything: the situations that arise, the actions we take, and the decisions we make. It's a monumental choice.

*I will be thoughtful about my choices today. If I want a good day,
I'll rely on the Holy Spirit.*

Relationships repeat themselves.

Who we encounter is never coincidental. Every person who crosses our paths is a potential learning partner or a temporary control-opponent. In one sense, they serve the same purpose. We share a mission *here,* and we will all complete it, eventually.

Some relationships strike us as hostile, not worth the effort to make them tolerable. More often than not, we learn the most from them. Why is that? No doubt it's because we have to give up our attempts to change them and pray for acceptance. It shouldn't surprise us that when we pray for a different understanding of someone or something, we get it.

We are learning that how we see one person influences how we see everyone else. Perhaps we hadn't noticed that before, but if we were prone to judging someone, we quite easily fell into judging, at least on a small scale, even those we claimed to love fully. It might be said that we really have only one relationship in this entire experience of life. Healing it will heal them all.

*I will take the opportunity to heal every relationship
by deciding to teach only love today.*

Forgiveness

 We are ensnared by an illusory world.

How do we know that what we see is not real? There is a simple test: ask, "Does it change, ever, in any way?" If it does, it's not eternal; it's not real. This is important because the ego gets invested in trying to change, to our liking, other people and numerous situations every day. Each resulting conflict moves us further from peace, from the Real World. The Holy Spirit wants to return us to God and home when we are ready. Readiness is nurtured through our expressions of love.

How can we refrain from reacting angrily to the circumstances around us, particularly when they are affecting us negatively? What the *Course* tells us is that nothing can affect us without our assent. What we have to do to withdraw the assent is seek the peace within, seek the comfort of the Holy Spirit's presence. It's waiting in the quiet place of our minds for our invitation to guide the response.

Forgiveness is the single most sensible response to every circumstance today. I will experience the Real World within if I comply.

Problems exist only in the mind.

When we've missed an airplane, sprained an ankle, or lost a bill-fold, we're not easily convinced that problems exist only in our minds. Surely we're not supposed to deny all the mishaps that plague us.

It's true, unfortunate events happen. When they do, we must acknowledge them, take responsibility for getting back on track, then move on. We have the capacity to look beyond them and realize they are teaching tools rather than catastrophes. Nothing has to hinder our growth. Every experience can be a way to draw closer to the Holy Spirit and thus God.

Knowing that we can "manufacture" acceptance and even joy at will changes every element of our lives. This, in turn, can help to change the lives of those close to us. How we treat them can be contagious.

How I see a situation today determines the outcome.

October 18

Choice

 The world we choose to see costs us our peacefulness.

It seems improbable that we'd conjure up scenes of famine and destruction by choice. Yet that's what we're told as students of the *Course.* Are we to ignore the devastation and violence we see everywhere, burying our heads in the sand? It may seem so when we first get involved with these teachings, but that's missing the point. The *Course* merely says we see what the ego creates. If we want to see something else, we can. When we choose the perspective of the Holy Spirit, we'll create scenes of love.

This sounds simplistic. However, we have little familiarity with relying on the Holy Spirit rather than the ego for our perspective. Most of us didn't even know both options existed until recently. We can't be expected to change instantly how we see the world around us. Still, to practice choosing peace-filled scenes can't hurt us. It's certainly worth the effort to have a different experience of one's life.

My eyes will see what I desire today.

*Death has no power unless we
choose to identify with it.*

There's nary an advertisement on television or in a magazine that doesn't encourage us to buy a look-and-stay-young product. Although we don't readily acknowledge this, we are, of course, trying to eliminate the aging process, which is one small step away from death. How can it possibly be true that death has no power over us? Don't funerals, cemeteries, and final will and testaments all testify to how real death is?

While we're engaged *in this world*, it's obvious that death is a reality. But the *Course* helps us see that only the body dies, and the body is nothing more than a vehicle the ego has created to carry us through this panorama of experiences. When we've learned the truth, we'll discard the body. The body will die, but our real self will not. We can think about death in a new way now. Indeed, death has no power over who we are and what we do.

*I am in charge of my life! Today invites
my full involvement.*

Real World

 *We glimpse the Real World in the instant
we choose not to be afraid.*

Perhaps we wonder how something so elusive as the Real World is attainable so effortlessly. The avenue to it, of course, is our disavowal of fear. And that disavowal is nothing more than our decision to walk with the Holy Spirit rather than the ego.

The ego wants us to be afraid. The ego holds us hostage, pitting us against the men and women we have chosen as our Teachers. This world is our classroom, but that doesn't mean we are stuck here against our will. We can *depart* in a moment's notice, for a long period or simply an instant at a time. The departure is what's important. It will change the dynamics of our relationship with each of our Teachers every time we make it.

It's pretty exciting to contemplate how free we are to "create" the kind of day we want to experience. If we want tension or fear, it's ours. If we'd rather enjoy peace, we can count on that too. The Real World, the "home" of eternal peace, is merely an eye-blink away.

Today I can choose peace over fear.

We are here as Teachers of God.

When we question our purpose, we have only to remember our role as Teachers. If we're new on this path, we may misinterpret "Teacher." We may feel too insecure or vulnerable to harbor any notion of teaching others. The truth, however, is that we are teaching others every waking moment. Our actions and words, our body language and facial expressions, continuously tell others who we are and what we want them to know. These qualities reinforce what we think as well.

Keeping this in mind can inspire us to monitor what we teach. We'll discover that we will become more comfortable teaching only love. We will come to genuinely care for one another's soul. Ultimately we will learn that responding in a loving way to every circumstance will foster a nurturing outcome.

*God has given me the Holy Spirit as a partner
for all my work today.*

Problems

 Christ cannot deny a call for help.

How many times a day do we ponder what decision is right regarding a friend in pain or a sticky problem with a neighbor or at work? Far too often we limit the search for a solution to the dictates of the ego. We always have another option available through Christ.

Many of us resist seeking help from Christ because of our childhood experiences. How can we get over our resistance? The best way is by asking the very entity we're resisting for help in seeing Him in another way. If we want a new perspective, we'll get it.

I can count on help if I ask for it today.

Let's join with one another.

Looking at our companions as "others," as separate human beings, can make us defensive and insecure. Considering how quickly arguments are triggered and feelings are hurt, it's not easy to grasp that we are One in the Real World. Feeling compassion for anyone who is hurting will heighten our awareness of Oneness.

When we are lonely, afraid, or anxious, we can gather a moment's peace along with hope from a friend who "joins" us by reaching out. He or she doesn't even have to speak. Just knowing that our problem matters to someone else lessens it for us.

Sharing our burdens with the people who reach out to us gives them a chance to show love. We are teaching and learning simultaneously. We strengthen each other and enhance all the dreamed-for possibilities of our lives. We can do so much for one another's happiness every day with so little effort.

*I will look for an opportunity to join
forces with another soul today.*

All relationships can be holy.

We are involved in many relationships: co-workers, neighbors, family members. Some relationships are more enjoyable and nurturing than others, but that shouldn't surprise us.

What makes some of them good and some not so good? The level of quiet peace we feel while in the presence of some people is a strong indication of which are good. We feel in tune with some people, not competitive, mistrusting, or superior to, but rather warmly alike. We have decided, consciously or unconsciously, to join with those individuals and thus are walking a common path.

What about the relationships in which we feel trapped? We can't switch jobs, perhaps, or move to a new neighborhood. How can we tolerate the seemingly harmful relationships? The *Course* and our Teachers suggest we seek points of commonality with the people in those troubled relationships. They are there, we're assured, or they wouldn't be on our path.

I can do my part to create a holy relationship today where one didn't exist yesterday.

There are no coincidences.

It's reassuring to hear that we are exactly where we need to be. It's even more reassuring to know that we will be drawn toward those people who have much to teach us. We can live free of worry if we suspend our fear and judgments and simply trust that we're moving in the right direction all the time.

This doesn't mean that we won't take a detour occasionally and end up in a hurtful situation. But we'll recognize, instantly, that we got off course. When this happens, the solution is to ask the Holy Spirit for help and a new direction. One will come to us. In the meantime, we have an opportunity to practice the principles of the *Course* by offering love even though it's not immediately returned.

Wherever we are, we have "work" to do. And the job is always the same. The uncertainty that plagued us for so many years is gone forever. We have heard the call and we are its messengers.

*I am in the company of the people who
need me most today.*

Choice

We try to adjust to the world we made.

Might there be a better world than the one we're experiencing, a place free from violence and poverty, abuse and disease? The answer, of course, is yes. The *Course* teaches that we have created *this* world of experiences, and if we want something different, that's up to us.

It's not coincidental that we have crossed the paths of our companions. We have decided we want what we experience together or we would have created something quite different. This knowledge allows us to feel both grateful and responsible. It also pushes us to return to the drawing board if we want a different world.

It's folly to settle for what we experience if it leaves us unhappy or dissatisfied. The better world is always a mere thought and decision away. Our companions will be there too. Let's not try to fit into a world we don't like.

*My mind is my tool for happiness today. It will follow
the Holy Spirit's lead if I choose that voice.*

*The outer world mirrors our inner thoughts
in every instance.*

We make whatever we see, plain and simple! If we're not happy, the responsibility lies with us to make something else, and we can do this in an instant by changing our thoughts.

As novices to the *Course,* we may find it difficult to change our minds. A tiny bit of practice, on the other hand, reveals how easy it is. So what if we have to keep "changing our minds." Every time we replace a negative thought with one of love or peace, we'll feel relief. We'll also feel empowered and hopeful in every situation we encounter.

It's not easy to understand how thought projection works. Perhaps we don't have to. But believing in the principle and then thinking only love demonstrates how what we think reflects back to us. How we see others changes forever when we embrace this principle.

*Reflecting on love and God today will emphatically
change my experiences.*

October 28

There is only good in the Real World.

If a basic attribute of the Real World is that only good happens there, most would agree we don't live there on a daily basis. That's not an easy idea to embrace. Where are we then? What is *this* world? And even more important questions are where, if not here, is the Real World, and how do we get there?

When we're told the Real World is simply in our minds, many are still confused. To whom do we go for understanding? If we're fortunate enough to be in a *Course* study group, we can seek guidance there. It's not coincidental that we have been brought together to share this experience. Among any circle sit Teachers as well as students.

We are learning that when we invite the Holy Spirit to interpret our experiences, we'll see only good. And when we let the Holy Spirit determine our actions, we will do only good. Any other interpretation, any other response, evolves from the ego's worldview. Let's stay in the Real World and know peace.

I am free to live in the Real World or the ego's world today.
My choice defines everything.

Hurtful actions

As God's children we cannot be hurt.

If we are God's children, thus can't be hurt, how are the injuries we or others experience explained? What about the abandonment we suffer when a spouse leaves or a friend rejects us? We can all recall times when either we or someone close to us suffered grave physical or emotional injuries. Aren't we all God's children?

Of course we are. And yet, every moment that we let the ego take command of our lives, we are not protected from harm. The ego knows only attack, thus it initiates only attack. The hurts pile up and more hurts are instigated. It's a vicious cycle that is as short-lived as we will it to be. Our job is to seek an alternative to any ego-inspired action and let God, through the Holy Spirit, inspire a loving approach. It's a simple solution to an aggravating situation.

If I feel hurt by someone's actions today, I'll seek another way to see the experience. There is one, always.

October 30

Negative thoughts

 Let's not fear our impure thoughts.

It's important to remember that every thought we harbor is self-generated and no thought is independently powerful without our acquiescence. While it's true that many of our thoughts, every day, are wholesome and loving, a few are mean-spirited and can lead to regret. When they mirror the latter, we have momentarily succumbed to the ego's control. That's problematic, temporarily.

We don't have to honor any impure thought. It's equally true, and maybe disturbing, that we don't have to honor the good ones either. At least it's fortunate that we are selecting friends who share our current spiritual journey and desire for more love and peace in their lives.

It's easier to make any new, positive behavior or way of thinking habitual when you surround yourself with role models who do likewise. But even when we sit among the naysayers, we don't have to give our minds to the ego. Perhaps it's our job, at that moment, to be the role model for everyone else.

My nasty thoughts are no stronger than I make them.
Today is open to my interpretation.

Death is not real.

What can it mean that death is not real? We look around and see dying plants every day. We've no doubt been to many funerals and have had many discussions about death with friends and family. How can we believe that something which captured our attention and participation so significantly is not real? Are we all insane? The unexpected response is, yes. We are.

Most of us need a more elaborate explanation though. Death only appears to be real in this illusory world, which the *Course* tells us isn't real. We've created it as a silly act of defiance and now, with the ego's help, we preserve it. Because it isn't finally real, nothing we see here lasts. Thus, death seems to occur. The illusion is therefore supported.

What does any of this matter? Do we really care what's real and what isn't? If we want to get back home, if we want to experience real peace and joy, it does matter that we understand this principle. The easiest path to understanding it is to seek God's help. We know where that's found, don't we? All things will become clear when we are ready for the answers.

If someone speaks to me of death today, I'll listen, instead, to the Holy Spirit's voice.

NOVEMBER

Salvation is the miracle of right choosing.

The ideas in the *Course* offer us salvation from the pain and conflict that arise every instance that the ego takes charge of our lives. Choosing to let the Holy Spirit direct our thinking and our actions saves us from unnecessary and unenlightening pain.

Why would anyone ever choose to forego the miracle? It's certainly not done with foresight. But when we're still taking baby steps along this new spiritual path, we can't see what lies ahead. It's only after enduring the mistakes from our choices that we understand the ramifications. The idea of control seduced us until we realized the extent of our imprisonment.

Freedom from pain, anxiety, uncertainty, and fear is the miracle we are guaranteed if we make the simple, right choice repeatedly. It's easy to seek the insight of the Holy Spirit.

*My peacefulness is in jeopardy today unless
I turn a deaf ear to the ego.*

November 2

Resistance

The Course *is alien to all that we've believed before.*

When we try to tell others what we are learning in *A Course in Miracles,*® we're often met with resistance. Most people aren't comfortable with an extremely different worldview. Saying that the world we think we're experiencing is not the Real World, sounds far-fetched. It may have sounded that way to us in the beginning too.

Leaders of *Course* study groups often suggest that we not try to educate those who aren't ready. But after learning that we aren't separate from them, that we are all One, that notion seems odd too. How do we make sense of all this? Let's ask for a different vision and wait for it to come. We are promised peace if that's what we want. All we have to be willing to do is get quiet rather than try to create solutions to problems that we don't understand.

If I have trouble explaining how I think today, I'll give up the attempt and offer love and acceptance instead.

Problems have no life of their own.

When we're in the midst of emotional pain, it's not easy to believe that problems reflect only the life we give them. Why would we want experiences such as these?

The truth, of course, is that we create problems in an attempt to assuage our own guilt, the guilt we have for our perceived imperfections. What we dislike in ourselves, we relish seeing in other people. And when we do, we often attack them, or at least react in some judgmental, unloving way. What's the way out of this insidious cycle? Lucky for us, there is one.

We do see only what we choose to see. If we decide we want to see only the good in other people and situations, we will. Obviously this means we can see only our perfect self too, the same self that God sees. We don't need problems in our lives, ever. While some say we learn from them, and that may be true, we can complete our journey without them if we so choose.

I will be problem-free today, unless I choose otherwise.

November 4

Illness

 Every physical ailment arises in the mind.

We may have experienced doctors who have implied an illness was in our heads. We felt discounted, maybe hurt by their insensitivity. It's not likely their diagnosis came from an understanding of *A Course in Miracles.*® However, what they said was correct. Little by little, we are coming to understand this. All illness is mental illness.

This is good news, really. If sickness isn't real, if it's only in the mind, it can be healed by changing the mind. Many wonder if this means a cure is inevitable. That may happen, in fact. But the healing, the miracle, is a shift in how one perceives his or her condition. The so-called sickness may remain, but how it affects one's life is totally different. When we aren't attached to the body and its illness, it loses its importance for us. The freedom we feel changes how we see everything else that's happening around us too.

I am lucky that illness need not control my life. How I see it
or anything else that's occurring is my decision today.

Forgiveness makes us peaceful.

Few would claim to want turmoil or stress in their lives. And yet, that's what most of us have daily. We want situations to be different, people to change, dreams to come true. We complicate our wants by trying manipulation and control, as directed by the ego, and conflict results instantly. Is there really another way to live?

The *Course* tells us there is another way. Jesus has shared that way with us through the text. To live peacefully every instant takes little more than a willingness to look beyond this illusion the ego has created. What the ego has intended is the turmoil we're experiencing. The ego is not the friend the Holy Spirit is. God did not give us the ego for guidance. God's gift was the Holy Spirit. Let's not forget, the Holy Spirit is just as available as the ego, and just as close. The decision is all that's different.

How peaceful do I want to be today?
I can make and remake my choice
as often as necessary.

Oneness

 Healing opportunities wear coats of many colors.

The men and women in our lives who are easy to love and forgive are less our Teachers than those we despise. We so much more easily and gratefully identify with the former. It's a most difficult lesson to understand that the more obnoxious traits in an associate are specifically present for us. Let's recall what this means.

The goal of this *Course* and any spiritual pathway, for that matter, is to become aware of the lie regarding our separation from God and one another. We never really left Heaven; we never actually separated from our Creator. The ego tells us otherwise, but that's because of its insanity. And it can only stay alive if it succeeds in pitting us against one another; thus, the anger or disgust we feel for a friend or a stranger is the ego's dirty work.

The important task for us is to see through the qualities we despise and realize the perpetrator of this perception is none other than ourselves. When we finally understand this, we'll be closer to realizing the Oneness that's been true all along. Our healing and our return home happen in tandem.

I will not be revolted by anyone today. With the Holy Spirit's help, I'll see people for who they really are.

*In the ego's thought system,
death is God's punishment.*

To transcend the ego's thought system, and thus the idea and fear of death, is one goal of the *Course*. Every day each experience is an opportunity to let the Holy Spirit formulate our thoughts and vision. When we choose that option, we'll feel free, awash with love. Death will never cross our minds when we live in the Holy Spirit's thought system.

Some may wonder what difference it makes whether we fear death or not. The difference is that the dread of death colors how we see and how we react to every person and event in our lives. When we determine our behavior on whether we'll be punished for it or not, we're not expressing unconditional love or forgiveness. The ego is bargaining with the people in our lives and we'll never know peace.

*The idea of death does not occur to me when I'm
expressing the love of God. I'll note how this
changes my experiences today.*

November 8

Separation

 Our separation from God is an illusion.

It is comforting to know that we were never abandoned by God. Nor have we ever left the security of His realm. We don't remember our life with God, but it was and is real. It's impossible to be, even now, where God is not.

Why doesn't this seem true? The only reasonable answer is that that's how cunning the ego is. Its survival is dependent on our alignment with it. Were we to remember God and acknowledge our Oneness with God, the ego would be doomed.

Can it really be that this world is only an illusion? We can touch objects, we can hear voices, we can interact with people in the same room and miles away. To be told this is illusory, not actually real, seems crazy. Let's look at it another way. We have opted for bodies as our vehicles to move through this classroom. And on this level, everything we see is real. But the Spirit within our body, and everyone else's too, is all that's actually real, nothing more.

I am at home with God today. Nothing has to upset my enjoyment of this fact.

True Self
Grace

When we remember who we are we know grace.

A difficult *Course* principle says the bodies we see are not the whole of us. The *Course* is reintroducing us to our basic spiritual cores.

Initially, this idea confuses all students. It's best if we just take on faith that there is more to us than we currently know. It helps if we remember a time in our past when we were spared the awful consequences of a dangerous circumstance. Somehow we were guided to safety. That connection we felt with this guiding force is who we really are.

We are the embodiment of God, even though we seldom sense it. Fortunately, we can develop a better sense of it if we quietly seek it, and when we feel the Oneness, which is guaranteed to happen, the peace, the grace, and who we really are will be known.

If I am troubled today, I've forgotten my real identity.
All I have to do is seek to know it and I will.

We will be told all we need to know.

We all wonder how to respond to unfavorable conditions. Before coming to the *Course,* we often were frantic when making decisions. We were certain we had to be right, which filled us with fear. The fear, in turn, kept us from feeling and expressing love, which would have unmistakably guided us rightly.

It's a simple idea, yet so hard to grasp, that we are either feeling love or fear at every moment. We don't always recognize fear, however. Sometimes it looks like anger, resentment, sadness, or disappointment. Acceptance of how love and fear operate in our lives will speed our growth and understanding. It will also bring us peace.

The Holy Spirit is as close as our thoughts. With Its help (and all we have to do is ask for it) we can evaluate our lives through eyes that see only love.

I don't have to wonder what to do today.
The Holy Spirit is waiting to tell me.

Love for one is love for all.

We simply don't express pure, unconditional love. Even when we think we love someone, the ego has imagined a scenario that "pictures" a certain response from them. Real love expects nothing. The ego resists relinquishing expectations.

How can we ever attain the state of feeling absolute love for another person? By ourselves, we can't. The ego has too much at stake to bow out quietly. We do have a tool at our disposal that can create the love we'd like to express, however. We have to get quiet to use it, and that's not always easy. The ego is loud and intimidating, but perseverance pays off. The Holy Spirit wants to respond to our call for help. We simply have to ask. The miracle is that when we do feel love, total love for one, it touches everyone else.

My feelings of love for one person affect how I feel about everyone. All my relationships will be helped today by my love for one.

November 12

Anger

Anger cannot bring us what we want.

How do we get trapped into thinking anger has value for us? Even a cursory glance at the shelf of self-help books in a local bookstore provides one answer. It's a popular topic for authors. It's certainly not uncommon for therapists to counsel people to deal with their anger. Many go so far as to say that anger has to be expressed to whomever *caused it* for it to go away. We're also told that anger can serve us. In light of all this, it's not surprising that we struggle with the *Course* idea that anger never serves us well.

Each of us must devise a way to change our thinking that fits us personally; however, there are some suggestions that can help everyone. We can reflect on even the most recent time we got angry and genuinely evaluate its effect on the people or the situation. Did they willingly change? Did we feel at peace with the outcome? Let's never forget the noneffectiveness of anger. We can also ask the Holy Spirit to help us feel forgiving and show us another way to see the person or the situation that triggered our outburst. The Holy Spirit will guide us, every time.

My anger never has to last or be expressed. If I feel an attack coming on today, I have the ready help of the Holy Spirit.

*We have the power to strengthen
our willingness to love.*

Most of us have numerous characteristics that we don't relish. We are pretty ashamed of some, in fact. Isn't it interesting that we note these same traits in others? What a relief. We're not the only "sinners." Often we decide that someone else displays the trait in even more obnoxious ways than we do. That's really good!

The ego is out of control in such cases. It can't see the truth, the Oneness of all. It recognizes nothing but the negative aspects of others because single-handedly it projects them. The ego never loves or forgives or is at peace, so it can't see goodness in others. Only what lies *within* a thought manifests *without*.

Committing to see only love in the external world will be answered with only love in return. It's a perfect balance, always. What we get, we have given. Who we see, we are. The only way we can change our experiences in the outer world is by thinking from the peace-filled side of our inner world.

*If I want more love in my life, I have to
cultivate my willingness to forgive.
Today will test my willingness.*

Control

 *When the ego is threatened we can expect a battle—
an inner one or an actual one with a companion.*

What is a threatened ego? It's when the ego feels like it's losing control of a situation or some person. The fear of this happening is so overwhelming that the ego attacks whoever is present, sometimes relentlessly. Does it maintain control through this process? Never, at least not for long. The cycle of conflict just keeps repeating itself with nothing gained.

The futility of this process drives some of us to finally ask, "Is there another way?" *A Course in Miracles®* has been offered as our answer. Let's be grateful that Bill Thetford posed the same question. We're the ones able to profit from the reply. *There is another way* and it's so simple. We seek another understanding of the circumstances or the people who seem to be the cause of our discontent. Our perceptions will change. Peace will surround us, providing we want it more than the seduction of control.

*If I am attracted to the idea of control at any time today,
I'll take note of it and seek a moment of peace instead.*

No special relationship works.

We are learning a whole new meaning for "special" since being introduced to the *Course*. The negative references to special relationships confuse us initially. To the ego, the special relationship is the only relationship, and the ego created it to meet its needs. What are those needs?

The ego seeks control and superiority over everyone. To do that, it has to attack and blame almost every person it encounters. The *Course* teaches that there is another kind of relationship. It's called the holy relationship.

In holy relationships we seek to see our Oneness with others; we seek to express only love. The joining of these souls allows for transcendence over the material obstacles created by the ego. A holy relationship "works." The participants in a holy relationship know God.

If I am caught in a special relationship today,
I'll remember I can make it a holy one.

Peace

 Knowledge is not the goal of the Course.
Peace is!

Knowledge has value, but it won't guarantee happiness if we continue to filter our experiences through the eyes of the ego. The ego's purpose is to push us to be more aggressive and controlling in all our relationships. Peace is never that outcome.

If peace is this *Course*'s goal, how can we be certain of attaining it? The steps to take are simple. Every encounter is an opportunity. First, when someone engages us in conversation, if we feel any inkling to judge them negatively, immediately ask the Holy Spirit to help us see them differently. Next, ask the Holy Spirit to give us the words to say or the feelings to project. Then wait for the words and the feelings to come. They will. Always. Our impatience may push us to act too soon, however. We'll have to be vigilant.

*I welcome all opportunities for knowing and
conveying peace today.*

We never really left the Real World.

When we hear that this is not the Real World, we are prone to ask, "Where is the Real World if not *here,* after all?" The answer is just as mysterious. The *Course* says we never actually left the Real World except in our minds, one part of our minds, in fact. Where we are now is in the company of the ego and the world it created. Because of the ego's hold on us, we have unwittingly blocked out the memory of the Real World. The truth is that the Real World is still very much alive although seemingly lost to us.

The way we typically look at the circumstances and the people around us, it's hard to believe that they aren't real, that they aren't all that exists. Many may not grasp this concept for years. That's okay. All we have to grasp, or at least accept, is the knowledge that what we see and who we see have been determined by the ego. If we want a different picture, we can't settle for the ego's world as our home.

Which world I inhabit today depends on my choice.
Only one world promises peace.

November 18

Purpose
Peace

It is inevitable that we will learn
what the Course *teaches.*

The ego says, "Why should we change?" And so we often go about our not-so-merry way attached to the ego and our argumentative stance to most situations. Eventually we discover acquaintances who are living more peaceful lives than we. When we begin to wonder why, we have begun the journey that will make our lives more serene too.

Coming to believe that all of us are destined to traverse this path in time makes the trip more intriguing. The basic teaching of the *Course* isn't necessarily new, nor is it unique. Many spiritual philosophies have suggested a similar way to live. What's interesting here is the emphasis the writings place on the idea that we will all eventually embrace the importance of love and forgiveness. Our opportunity is to help others find the path earlier by our example.

My job is easy today:
Think and give only love.

Every conflict experienced is caused by
one of two thought systems.

What does it mean to have two thought systems? Understanding this takes time. Initially we can't imagine why we'd need two. Isn't thinking simply thinking? But the thinking process is more complicated than we've credited it with being. The positive side of this is that we can choose which thought system to use.

If one system causes all the conflicts, why would we ever choose it? That's an intriguing consideration. It's hard to imagine a person wanting conflict; thus, it's hard to imagine one choosing that system of thought. But it happens. All the time. And most of us are the brunt of just such people every day.

Who are they? They are us, of course. They may look like our spouses or children or co-workers, but they are really us. Who we see and what we experience each day depends on what we think. Our desire to control how our lives unfold pushes us to select the ego's thought system. Conflict ensues. We get entrenched in it and create whatever transpires.

What do I want in my life today?
I can have it.
It's mine.

November 20

Perfect timing
Worry

 *We are always in the right place at the right
time to learn what we need to know.*

We worry far too much about how to *do* life! Have I prepared
enough for this assignment? Am I the right mate for this particular person? Did I offer the right example to those who look up
to me? We may have to stretch our willingness to believe that we
are exactly where we need to be all the time. But it's true.

The events of our lives are the classroom for our minds.
That's a refreshing idea. It saves us from regret over the past. It
gives us hope for the present and the future. The people with
whom we come together have something to offer us. If not love,
then the opportunity for us to offer it anyway. Every experience
is a time for healing. We are always the healers as well as the
healed. We are never where we can't be helpful to the others in
our midst.

␡

*I can overcome fear today if I remember
I am where I need to be.*

*We were created to be in Heaven,
not this world.*

Why are we here? The correct answer offers little solace. The *Course* says *we're not really here;* we only think we are. Confusing? Yes. But together we can understand it. First though, we have to accept on faith that God was the Creator and He is eternally present in Heaven. At one time, we were unified with God and nothing that we now see existed, but in an unexplainable moment, the ego was born and this nightmare evolved.

We are in this nightmare still. We can return to Heaven anytime we wish; however, the ego easily convinces us that nothing but this world exists. We have only the faintest recollection of the other world, and we only have it when we have tired of the ego's control and sought the refuge of the quiet within. Then and only then are we in touch with God, thus Heaven. In the quiet space of our minds, we can hear the humble voice of the Holy Spirit. We can listen to it if we want. We can experience peace, and we can be free of conflict and fear. Heaven is available now.

I experience Heaven today.

Relationships

Holy Relationships come from joining with another fully in the presence of the Holy Spirit.

Not every relationship is holy. But all of them can become holy if we see and revere the Spirit within each person. When this happens we stop looking for what we can get from the person and start looking for what we can give to the relationship. We know that loving acceptance and total forgiveness draw us together as One. Holiness lies therein.

The ego, in its need to control others, doesn't make room for the Holy Spirit. As a consequence, it forces relationships to be self-serving. The inherent tension and struggle that result restrict growth and prevent any sense of well-being. It's difficult to feel and offer love in a relationship that's mean-spirited.

It's fortunate and not accidental, that either person in a relationship can move it toward a holy one. The desire for peace and the willingness to forgive simply have to be greater than the wish to be right and in control.

I can help to make a relationship holy by my actions alone. Today is bound to offer me the opportunity I need.

The goal is to lose sight of our separateness.

The ego loves to keep us feeling separate from others at work, at home, in our families, in our social groups, everywhere. This is how the ego manages to control our thoughts and actions.

Feeling separate from anyone, anytime never nurtures us. We get obsessed with comparisons, feeling either inferior or superior. We can't experience love, our own or someone else's, when we are measuring ourselves against others. But how can we see beyond the separateness?

It's not accidental that we have begun to ask this question. Neither is it accidental that we are gravitating toward others who seek this answer too. The desire, the little willingness to be at peace with others, will move us closer to the Holy Spirit. And our feelings of separateness will begin to fall away.

Today I will remember that giving up my feelings
of separateness is a process.

Truth

 We are always moving toward the Truth.

It's possible to resist the knowledge that the Holy Spirit holds out to us; however, It will continue offering it to us anyway. At some point we will all be ready to seek a different understanding of how this world works. How fortunate that whenever we are ready, the Holy Spirit is present to help us.

What is this Truth we're seeking, even though we may not realize we're seeking it? It's the understanding that we aren't separate bodies with separate minds; we are united as One Spirit with our Creator. Only loving thoughts are true; everything else is an appeal for healing and help. And miracles are shifts in perception, only that.

If we're in doubt that we're moving toward Truth, let's ask the Holy Spirit for some indication. If we seek to feel differently about the people and the experiences in our lives, Its influence on our perceptions will change our feelings. It will take only a single instance to see this. We can choose to see it as often as we desire.

My destination today is Truth. I will reach it with the Holy Spirit's help.

The Holy Spirit is never wrong.

Most of the decisions we need to make require some consideration. We are frequently wont to ask friends' opinions before we
act. It's surely wise to seek the wisdom of others; however, the
only really wise voice which is always at our beck and call, is that
of the Holy Spirit. It will always know the answer to our
dilemma. It is confused by nothing; whereas, our friends are as
fallible as us, unless, of course, they have sought their response to
our question from the Holy Spirit.

It's comforting to realize that we can be certain of every
action we take if we've sought the guidance and then truly listened to the voice of the Holy Spirit. We don't ever have to feel
uncertain again. About anything. That may seem far-fetched but
it's nonetheless true. The choice to get the direction or the information we need is ours to make moment by moment. Let's not
get lulled into thinking the ego won't try to speak to us too. It
will, of course. But the decision to listen only to the Holy Spirit
isn't that difficult to make, particularly when we remember the
results of taking the ego's direction on some occasion in the past.

*Any decision I make today can be the absolute right one if I've
sought the wisdom of God. What a comforting thought this is.*

Healed mind

 The healed mind knows only love.

Why do we have this need for healing? The explanation is not satisfying. We're told that in a moment of insanity, our separation from God *seemed to occur*. In reality, we never really left, but the ego thinks otherwise. The ego was the culprit then and it remains so. It knows only fear, thus when we listen to it, we know only fear. The ego's voice is loud because it wants control. Some days we can hear no other voice. Some days healing isn't even imaginable.

But we want to be healed. We want to return to the peace and love of God's world. Not surprisingly, we can help each other. That's why we're gathered here, now. Our offering of help is our expression of love and forgiveness. We each need both in this world. Healing only comes when love is all we know. The more we give, the more we'll receive.

I can help my mind heal today by sending out love to everyone I encounter.

*Separate interests are relinquished
in holy relationships.*

Even the most casual of experiences with other human beings are not without reason, not accidental. When we first come to the *Course,* this seems like a silly idea. How can the chance encounters on the bus or at the grocery really matter? But they do.

Likewise, the horrendous experiences have played their part, drawing us to another person for a lesson we each need. When the outcome has been violent, we abhor the idea that it served a purpose. How can our "education" be so intentionally painful?

What we are struggling to learn is that no encounter has to be painful. Problems result when two egos collide rather than join. The option to join was always there but wasn't seen. The Holy Spirit was always available to give us another perspective. It just wasn't sought.

It helps to remember that we aren't our bodies. The Spirit is never injured by injustice. The more able we are to align with the Spirit, the less we'll encounter pain of any kind.

*I am as pain-free as I decide to be today.
Other people cannot hurt me
without my consent.*

Truth

Why are we afraid of the Truth?

It probably doesn't seem like we are afraid of the truth. In fact, we heap praises on Truth seeking, our own and others. But in the context of the *Course,* we are afraid of Truth. That's why we have created this hostile, violent, and sometimes indifferent world.

The key question, of course, is what's there to be afraid of? Our answer is, the wrath of God. In our ego-directed, insane minds we think we deserve to be punished for leaving the Real World. Our leaving killed God, we think, and now we have to pay. This "truth" will destroy us, so we have hidden from it.

The *Course* tells us a different story. We're told God still exists. We never really left His presence. We don't need this world of illusions we've created. They only serve to keep us from our real self and from God. There is nothing to fear "at home." Our memory of it *here,* if we can conjure one up, will make us peaceful and unafraid.

Today's truth is the same as yesterday's.
God does not wish us harm.
He waits for us to come home.

We can't adapt this world to us.

Wanting to change all the circumstances in our lives to meet our specifications is so commonplace. Not only do we want to change every detail, we willfully try to do so, and we butt heads with all the other egos who also try to control every event. Most days are riddled with conflict and we seldom meet with success. Opposing opinions aren't easily blended.

When we can't change the people and the situations in our lives, what comes next? Until we acquired the wonderful tool that is now at our disposal, we sulked or screamed; sometimes we withdrew and planned our revenge. What a refreshing response we're able to make now. And it's so simple. Funny that it never occurred to us before, but our entire identity was wrapped in our need to be right, to be in control. Can we really part with that need?

Deciding to seek another way to see the struggle we're in removes the stress and the burden of whatever is happening. Only after trying this on many occasions do we come to fully appreciate how good life can be when it's just left alone.

Today is my chance to look for agreement with others.
I'll find it every time if I really want it.

Real self

 The Holy Spirit is the voice of our real self.

God placed the voice of the Holy Spirit within us when we left Him to remind us that we are not separate minds and separate bodies. We are all One with God. That He gave us the Holy Spirit as a companion during this illusory, nightmarish existence prevents us from totally forgetting who we really are. Whenever we let Its presence think for us, Its voice speak for us, Its heart act for us, we'll know the peace of being at home with God, the peace we left behind, the peace that's ours to return to at a moment's notice.

When we're trapped in the ego's mind, we can't imagine that there's another way to see and feel and act. The blessing is that we aren't trapped against our will. We are free to choose another perspective of every encounter we experience. Seeing the drama of our lives through the eyes of our real self changes who we think we are and, more important, who everyone else thinks we are. The excitement is just beginning. We can make this journey as full of hope, love, and peace as we make up our minds it should be.

*If I want to hear my real self today, I need only get quiet
and let the Holy Spirit's voice speak to me.*

DECEMBER

Problems

Living the Course *doesn't mean
having a problem-free life.*

We think we want to be problem-free. We're sure we don't need the anxiety and confusion that accompany all the unexpected situations in our lives. But struggles offer us opportunities to remember the presence of the Holy Spirit. Observing all experiences from Its view changes us, and our very lives, completely.

We can learn to accept our so-called problems as vehicles for the journey to serenity. Dreading them or responding to them with fear never comforts us. Quite the opposite, in fact. But this tiny change in mind-set changes how we experience all of life. How profoundly different we'll feel when we decide to rely on the Holy Spirit for our interpretation of the events of the day.

Practicing the presence of the Holy Spirit fills us with peace. We could have learned this long ago. Let's not waste any more time.

I will see anew today.

December 2

Truth

What we think we see is not the Truth.

We can only see what our minds project and, unless we are seeing solely from the perspective of the Holy Spirit, we are not seeing what is true. How do we know *who* is "seeing" for us? The answer is simple. If we are feeling peaceful and forgiving of all who cross our paths, our eyes are being focused by the Holy Spirit. If we feel fear or agitation, if we are harboring thoughts of attack, the ego is standing watch.

Occasionally we wonder if we'll ever wholly understand the *Course's* message. How can things we touch not be real? It helps to remember that our bodies serve solely as our vehicles for this journey we're making to Enlightenment. They have no other purpose. One day they will die, existing no more. Are they real? The same is true for all material objects. They aren't eternal, changeless entities. Only our Oneness with God is real and eternal.

When I look upon my world today, I'll seek to see beyond what the ego projects.

Guilt

Do I really wish to see others as sinless?

When we contemplate this question, we have to remember that how we see ourselves is how we see others. So the more accurate question is, "Do I wish to see myself as sinless?" Most would reply, "Of course." But is that really true?

Generally speaking, we are haunted by guilt for having left God and the Real World. We suspect we deserve to be punished for this act. Our self-hatred is assuaged slightly by condemning everyone else for their departure.

The relief this offers is extremely brief and superficial. But there is another way to think. The *Course* teaches us we are One with others; we are joined. It's possible to feel only love and acceptance. Can these ideas change our whole existence? Our Teachers say yes. Proof follows action.

When I feel bad about myself,
I want to bring others down too.
Then my guilt is doubled.
Today I won't do this!

December 4

 What kind of relationships am I cultivating?

The *Course* says there are two kinds of relationships: *special* and *holy.* The labels don't draw much distinction between them, but we discover they are radically different. Most of us searched for special relationships before embarking on this journey. Being devoted to someone and, better yet, having him or her devoted to us, was an all-consuming challenge, but the pain of success confused us. How could getting what we sought make us so unhappy?

We are learning that relationships that are special become possessive; they aren't good for us. Because we fear abandonment, which comes from our misinterpretation *that God left us,* we cling tightly to our companions. Every step they take that isn't directed by us makes us fearful, and our desire to hold on becomes an attack.

The good news is that holy relationships are so much easier. All that's required is the willingness to give up our judgments, to give only love. We have no hard decisions to make in the holy relationship. Just show up and be loving.

I'll evaluate all my relationships today.
If one needs changing, they all do.

Anger never benefits us.

We've been told that we must express our anger, and that it's necessary to confront whomever is responsible for it. From the *Course* we are learning something quite different. We are learning that anger is the ego on the loose. Anger is never necessary; it is always a cry for healing and help.

What does it mean when we are the brunt of someone else's anger? Shouldn't we at least address it? The *Course* says no. To address it is to make it real, which fosters its manifestation again and again. Our better response is to turn the other cheek, to offer loving forgiveness. Let's not forget that whatever we perceive in the experiences we've attracted directly reflects what we expected, what we projected, and what we actually wanted, even though we may insist otherwise.

No doubt we've all heard someone say, "But anger energizes me." Let's suggest they weigh the long-term results of the empowerment gained when they say no to anger and yes to love. How good it feels to take charge of our expressions.

Anger may try to imprison me today, but I hold the key that opens the door to freedom and peace.

December 6

Violence

This world is our classroom.

Turning on the news when we arise or scanning the daily newspaper makes us want to hide under the covers many mornings. Has this world gone crazy? The tragedies that befall people seem to be multiplying. Is this really true, or is the media's incessant focus on negative occurrences making them seem to proliferate? Regardless of our opinion on this matter, we all have to decide how to feel regarding the people and the situations we're apprised of. That's where the *Course* can play an important role.

What it tells us is that we need place no real importance on even the most horrific situation. In every instance it reflects insane egos. To respond to the madness with anything but forgiveness in our hearts is to exaggerate it. Fortunately, we do have the power to initiate healing in every troubling situation. Even when we aren't specifically involved, we can make a contribution toward the healing by how we choose to treat every person we encounter every day.

Nothing that is happening around me has to negatively affect me. In fact, I can perform a beneficial service for everyone by expressing only love to every person I see or even think about today.

We teach what we are ready to learn.

Our experiences serve as our tools for self-enlightenment. In the past we were invested in being right, winning arguments, and getting our way. Occasionally we got what we wanted, but the gratification never lasted long. That baffled us.

Not much has changed in the externals of our lives, yet it all seems very different now. The trigger? This new way of seeing. This tiny change has had a phenomenal impact. Seldom are we willing to push for a fight. We honestly would rather be peaceful than right.

Understanding that we have a sensible purpose in this life makes everything we do more meaningful. Our tasks don't have to be spectacular. We don't have to be superstars at anything. Just being the embodiment of love and peace is as big a job as we need.

I am teaching every minute. The plan is simple:
Today I will love everyone.

December 8

Healing

We all are healers.

The miracle of healing, according to this course of study, is simply the decision to shift our perceptions of the people and the experiences surrounding us. None of us has greater healing power than anyone else. Some practice the healing process more often, however.

The one absolute in every day for everybody is that there will be an opportunity to offer a healing gesture to someone or some situation. Just knowing that we can improve the world we live in by a tiny thought or action gives the most mundane of days real meaning. We are equal in our ability to move us all closer to home.

If we look at our experiences from this perspective, it will change how we see every minute of our lives. We'll even begin to look for opportunities to offer healing. Knowing that all of us benefit through the gestures of any one of us inspires our willingness to participate in the miracle.

I have the opportunity to add to the richness of every person's experience today through my perspective.

Any problem I have is in me, not someone else.

We love to blame others for every stumbling block that confronts us. Either our parents reprimanded us too much, or they were distant and uncaring. Perhaps our teachers pushed us too hard or mocked our mistakes. The kids in our classrooms and neighborhoods certainly had ample opportunities to fill us with fear and self-doubt. The list grows in proportion to our desire to blame someone else for every challenge in our life.

Eventually, with the help of the *Course,* we realize that blaming others is not the solution to how we feel. No situation, past or present, changes just because we have pointed the finger at someone else. On the contrary, as long as we avoid taking responsibility for our lives, we will fail to find genuine happiness. Putting our lives in the hands of anyone but the Holy Spirit guarantees we'll get only what they want for us, not what we desire for ourselves.

Claiming responsibility for our problems allows us to claim responsibility for our successes too. We are learning that by seeking the help of God, we'll have lots more of the latter.

*Along with the Holy Spirit, I am in charge of
what happens to me today.*

Faults

 Let's look upon our faults without judgment.

Everyone has faults. We wouldn't be here, *in this world,* if we didn't have something to learn. The mistakes we make, the defects we embody are our opportunities for growth and change. We are not being judged by God because of our imperfections, nor is the Holy Spirit keeping score. Only the ego perpetually judges us or anyone else.

Learning to stop passing judgment takes some effort. It seems second nature to us. Of course, that's exactly what the ego has in mind. Giving up judgment means vigilant monitoring of our thoughts and the willingness to replace negative thoughts with more loving ones. What we gain in the process is freedom from the guilt the ego foists on us every time we do its nasty bidding.

Acknowledging our faults and moving on gets rid of them far more quickly than dwelling on them in hopes that they'll leave. School is in session; let's not tarry.

I am not a hostage to any fault I still have.
My freedom from it rests within my mind.

Relationships never really end.

Relationships are eternal. This can be a comforting idea, particularly when a loved one dies and we want to savor the good memories and hold his or her Spirit close.

But what does it really mean to accept that our pain-filled, troubled relationships are also eternal? Some principles of this path are hard to rejoice over. The bottom line, however, is that each relationship is a teaching/learning opportunity. Each one helps us know the Spirit better. Each one offers a channel to the Holy Spirit, yet each one can trigger the ego if we're not vigilant.

If relationships never end, does it mean that we will again meet up with those we loved as well as those we loathed? The *Course* says yes. In some form we will come together again. And as Spirits we will know love; we will know how to offer only love. We will have rejoined God.

A difficult relationship is my opportunity
to look to the Holy Spirit rather than
being a hostage to the ego today.

December 12

Conflict

*Not all relationships that are right
for us are peaceful.*

Every person we have contact with offers a learning opportunity. It may happen that what we have to learn in some relationships doesn't feel all that pleasant. Even hostile relationships can be purposeful and valuable. Our mission is to heal, and healing occurs through our encounters with others.

It's not unusual to be confronted with the same difficult person day in and day out. The *Course* would say that's not coincidental. The agitation we feel is not about the other person, no matter how strong we desire it to be so. That we come together, again and again, can only mean healing is called for, and healing is possible. Our task is to desire it, seek a new perspective on the struggle, and wait. If we really want help, it will come. If we really want healing, it will happen.

*Today may include some strife with a friend.
We can draw closer if we so desire.*

Home is in our minds.

The *Course* teaches that no one goes home until we all go home. That means we are, in fact, One; what happens to one happens to us all. It makes sense to cultivate feelings of forgiveness and love, because projecting these positive feelings onto others teaches them to do likewise.

The difficulty is that we don't feel loving all the time. When we're caught in the throes of the ego, we experience lack, not love, and we seek what we lack from someone else. Because we mirror ourselves "out there," we do not discover the love we crave. Our existence becomes an insane cycle of lack causing more lack.

The cycle can be ended, however. That's the blessing. It's not difficult either. We can quietly rest the zealous ego and acquire the peace of the Holy Spirit. That peace is *home,* ultimately. And it's no further away than the blink of an eye. When we reside there more often, others will follow our example. We will all get home together.

I can be home in my quiet mind today.
My presence there will appeal to others too.

December 14

Old values

 Every value we held before must be discarded.

A Course in Miracles® can be described as radically different from most belief systems we've experienced. It's not easy to discard how we viewed the world before. Much of what we believed mirrored what our families taught us. Most of us struggle when trying to handle the knowledge that our families were wrong. Perhaps we can look at this in a different way.

Each of us has a role to be a purveyor of *Course* ideas. We teach by example. We don't have to force others to change; we don't even have to suggest that their way is wrong. All we need to do is live our own lives mirroring these new beliefs, letting others choose whether or not to mimic our example.

If we truly believe that we aren't separate minds and separate bodies, we'll be comfortable just *being,* not preaching. And we'll know that whatever we believed before was fine and that what we believe now is what we've been readied to learn.

An old value may rear its head today.
That's okay. I can smile on it
and go about my business.

How can I know God's will for me?

How commonly we fret trying to decipher God's will for us. We make the search quite complicated. We ask first one person and then another what we should do, and then we second-guess the suggestions. We generally evaluate them according to their benefits for us personally and discard ideas that aren't self-serving. The net result is seldom the peace we deserve, the peace that is truly God's will for each of us.

We can make our search easy. All we ever need to do is ask ourselves one question: "Is what I'm about to do or say or think a loving expression?" If the answer isn't yes, we are not fulfilling God's will. And every time we offer love to a friend or stranger, we are. Knowing, as we now do, what God's will for us is every minute promises us the peace we so much deserve. Our changed demeanor will contribute to the peacefulness of everyone else too.

*God's will is no mystery. If I want to live it today,
my assignment is easy. Give only love.*

December 16

Holy instant

A holy instant changes our entire perspective.

When we experience a *holy instant,* everything changes. How we see our companions, the way we interpret the events surrounding us, the expectations we have for the future are all affected by a holy instant. So let's review what it is.

The complete joining of two souls is a holy instant. But what does *joining* mean? It's that moment when we see, with profound clarity, our absolute Oneness with another human being. In that moment we realize how totally aligned we truly are. The fear of differences, the suspicion of separation are gone, absolutely. Our Oneness is all that we can feel and see and know.

In the holy instant we are at perfect peace. We are momentarily rejoined with God in the Real World we left before. We can return there at will. All we have to do is seek only peace and then express only love to our companions.

*I can create a holy instant at will. Today can be
an adventure in holy instants.*

Illness is an appeal for healing and help.

There are so many levels of illness, and we know so many people who are sick. Surely the inoperable cancers can't be lumped with the mild case of flu or recurring toothache. But according to the *Course,* they are equal, and the ego has manifested them during a moment of fear. It may not have intended for the illness to progress to the terminal stage, but its focus on lack and separateness initiated the condition. Its obsession with it thereafter worsened it.

What should we do when in the company of one who is ill? Offer love, unconditionally and constantly. People in their Right Mind don't opt to be sick. Our sincere devotion when they feel least deserving of love can teach them of their worth. Only when they truly believe it will they be able to choose good health.

Knowing the truth about illness doesn't mean we will always choose health. What we can do, however, is be conscious of our choices. Better yet, if we need help, ask for it outright. It will come.

If I feel uneasy today, I am too far from God.

December 18

Patience
Solutions

 We will never be denied the help we need.

We have had far too many experiences that didn't evolve as we'd planned. The battles we have fought were often fruitless and very harmful. We may have even prayed about the situations seemingly to no avail. What we are coming to understand is that the ego led us astray. If the ego solicits help in prayer, the answer generally reflects the ego's mood rather than God's will.

In spite of the ego's incessant interference, the Holy Spirit really wants to channel God's message to us. It simply waits quietly for all the ego's attempts to fail so It can respond to our call. How patient is the Spirit. How patient is God.

Our task is to go to the right source for the solutions to our problems. Can we finally trust that the ego is never the solution? All the turmoil we've experienced probably should have been lesson enough, but if it wasn't, that's okay. Time is with us. Awareness will come.

I will know what I need to in time. Today will give
me an opportunity to learn something of value.

**Change
Giving**

*Whatever we give to another,
we give to ourselves.*

We feel bad after we have intentionally harmed or undermined the well-being of someone else. No doubt our mean-spiritedness went unnoticed by some, probably those who are more convinced of the rewards of offering only love to the world. How much more peaceful our path would be if we followed their example.

We don't have to make huge changes in our lives to begin feeling much better. One act, one moment at a time, will result in monumental changes before we know it. What can we do? We can smile, always, instead of frowning or pouting. We can say please and thanks every time we have an exchange with another. We can listen with our hearts rather than the ego. We can make the decision to stay silent if what we are about to utter isn't loving.

*I will remember today that
when I smile and listen,
change occurs.*

December 20

We will give up judgment.

How many times have we heard from friends and foes that we should use better judgment? Now the *Course* tells us to give it up. Is judgment a bad thing? Seeking guidance from other students on this matter will be helpful. What we'll learn is that judgment, if "dictated" by the Holy Spirit, will never be wrong. On the other hand, if the ego has defined the terms of judgment, those terms will be at the expense of other people, always. The ego knows only fear. Fear always demands negative judgment.

It's hard to believe that we can give up judging others. It's the first, automatic response we have when another person claims our attention. How cunning is the ego!

Rather than relinquishing all of our negative judgments, we can begin to revise how we respond to others. Realistically, every decision we make requires judgment of some kind, but when we hear the voice of the Holy Spirit rather than the ego, we offer only love. We begin to judge others as always worthy of love.

If my thoughts of others are not loving today,
I'll ask the Holy Spirit for better thoughts.

A healed mind is our choice.

With little difficulty we can recognize a paranoid mind or a terrified one. Observing someone's behavior quickly informs us whether or not their mind is disturbed. We can just as quickly distinguish a peaceful mind, one that we assume is healthy. The important question is, "How does one attain the latter?"

We can query the happy souls we meet and seek their formula for living. It's probable that many paths lead to *the state of joy.* This suggests that there are many ways to find peace. And for that, we can be glad. We don't have to become clones of those we admire; though picking up some cues to find more peace in our own lives makes good sense.

Those of us studying the *Course* are particularly lucky because we have a specific path we can travel that's guaranteed to heal our minds. We'll attain hours of peace and joy if we request to see our Oneness and join with others anytime we feel disturbed with a situation. Our minds will change. Healing is a choice.

I can tell immediately if my mind is healthy or sick by how I respond to others. Today I'll respond with love.

December 22

Problems
Worry

Bringing a problem to the light dissolves it.

Most of us have exaggerated even the simplest concerns by incessantly focusing on them. Our worry never dissipated them. When we were lucky, the demands in other areas of our lives forced us to relinquish our attention. Presto! The situation often "righted" itself. Why didn't we learn from that lesson?

The road we travel today has done for us what we couldn't do before. We know now that putting the light of the Holy Spirit on any problem offers us a different understanding of it. Even when we think a situation is bent on destroying us, we can discover freedom from it by a mere change in perspective. Was it hard to get to this realization? Not really. A little willingness was all we needed.

Unfortunately, discovering the payoff of a different vision doesn't mean we'll seek one every time we are in trouble. The grasp of the ego on our minds is simply too great, too seductive on occasion. It's advantageous that we journey with others who can help us remember the better way.

I am at the mercy of a struggle today only if I want to be.

Conflict

Our fears fuel conflicts.

Most of us will engender or encounter at least one disagreement every day. Unexpected situations easily engage the ego. Generally our companion, in that moment, has had the ego engaged too, and we're plunged into conflict before we realize it.

Conflict isn't absolutely bad. It can, in fact, be the stimulus for meaningful communication. What is necessary is for one or the other party to offer a sincere expression of forgiveness, and the discussion's tone may dramatically change. The parties become joined and healing is possible.

Our conflicts always attest to our fears, but why are we afraid so often? It's because we have forgotten our Oneness with others. We see only our separate bodies and sense our separate minds, and the comparisons follow. Within an instant, the ego creates reasons for disagreement. Isn't it time to hold the ego in check? Let's close the door to it. In turn, that opens the door to peace.

I don't have to feel shame about my conflicts with others.
I need only understand them to be
willing to discard them today.

Giving

Giving equals receiving.

There's no ambiguity in this statement. In fact, it makes clear what we'll experience moment by moment throughout our lives. The power it gives us is awesome. Why do we so often use this power to our detriment?

If we had only one response to all the situations in our lives, we'd have either peaceful lives or terribly chaotic, painful ones. Because we have two choices, the expression of love or the willfullness to attack, we can get a mixture of both. Even cursory observation would suggest that we vacillate between our two options.

There's no principle that demands we balance the scales between these two. If anything, the *Course* encourages us to choose only love. And if we did, we'd receive an abundance of it in return. What we give, we'll receive. We're in the driver's seat. If our experiences are generally painful, we need to shift gears.

The opportunity to attack others will arise today,
but I can choose to love them instead.

We embody the Christ.

What do we generally see when we look at each other? We see selfishness, greed, fear, anger, loneliness, pain. We see that which we project, that which we expect. Why don't we expect joy and peace and love?

The decision to change how we see the people in our midst is tiny, though quite profound. Because we feel so inadequate, so lacking, so unlovable, we are driven to bring others down to our level. They can't be better than we are, not for long anyway. How much happier we'd all be if we'd remember the vital fact of our existence: Christ lives within us all. Our recognition of this eliminates all but the loving perceptions of one another.

How can we incorporate this understanding in a practical way? The easiest method is to monitor what we're thinking about each other every minute. If it's not a thought we'd proudly share with everyone else, it probably needs to be discarded for one that's more loving. Methodically, we can change what we think and what we see. In the process, we'll change who we are.

*The Christ within us deserves acknowledgment.
I'll look for Him everywhere today.*

December 26

Material objects

*Understanding the valuelessness of
material objects takes time.*

Most of us grew up believing life was about acquiring objects.
Faster cars, more toys, bigger houses, better clothes. Now the
Course says these mean nothing.

It's not unusual to end up losing some things we had valued
when we begin living the *Course*. The loss teaches us to know this
lesson even though we may resist it at first. We need friends we
can turn to for support and clarity about our experiences if we're
overwhelmed by a loss. Our Teachers are everywhere. We merely
have to notice them.

If nothing we see has any meaning, why do we see it? Let's
not forget the role the ego still plays. Our passage here is about
seeing beyond or through the physical world to the love that is
God. It's a process and letting go of our attachment to material
things is our journey.

*Today I need not be in a hurry to give up things.
My awareness of love will
grow a bit every day.*

We will all share a common vision in the end.

Our destination is the same. No matter who we are, we are on a journey that's bringing us all together in the end. How can that be? We look so different. Our beliefs are often at odds. Our dreams for the future don't match. But the *Course* tells us, "We are going home, and no one gets there until we all get there."

We manage this shared journey by helping each other seek a holier vision of each experience that troubles one of us. On any one day, some one of us can see "the better way" more clearly than others. Thus, our assignment is to listen when we are stuck, to offer love and clarity when we feel it, to remain quiet when we can't say something helpful.

Knowing that we are ultimately headed in the same direction fosters trust in one another and can make us more willing to help others. Occasionally we still feel jealous and antagonistic, but that's because the ego hasn't yet been buried. Give us time.

I can help someone who has a cloudy perspective today.
My own will be enhanced likewise.

December 28

Perspective
Choice

*We are always demonstrating one
thought system or the other.*

When we're in a controlling mood, the ego is holding us hostage. When we're smiling and comfortably walking past the turmoil, we've given the ego the boot! Why would we ever choose the discomfort that tags along with the self-serving ego?

When we're angry or anxious, we can always tap into another thought system. We all have acquaintances who seem stuck in the ego's point of view. Being an example to them of *another way* is perhaps the best we can offer today. Since love and fear are the only expressions available to any of us, we can be vigilant about which one we'll embody.

The ego will continue to get us in trouble on occasion. After all, we are still human. Learning to live in concert with the Holy Spirit is a process, for some a longer one than for others. We have all the time we need.

*Who will I be today?
What a thrill knowing it's my choice.*

We see ourselves everywhere.

No matter where we are or whom we are with, we get constant visual reminders of our many qualities. We're often perplexed or maybe disgusted by some observations. And too willingly we gloat over another's obvious shortcomings, having forgotten that we share them. Must it always be true that what we see in someone else mirrors a part, however small, of ourselves? The answer, of course, is yes. The positive side of this information is that there's never any question about the changes that are called for in our behavior.

It's normal to feel overwhelmed by our personal inventory, particularly if we have decided there is little that's right with us. That's why it's also necessary to take note of others' admirable qualities. We also share them.

Developing a balanced view of who we are is possible. However, we can't let the ego do all of our viewing. Let's remember that we're here, in these bodies, to attend "school." Discovering one thing about ourselves, good or bad, means we are mastering our assignment. We need hope for nothing more.

I know so much more about myself than I think. If I feel confused today, I'll get some help by carefully watching a friend.

Unity

We are One with God and each other.

We struggle when we forget that we are One with others. The "separation" we perceive is merely a figment of our imagination, in fact, and gives rise to the fights, the fears, the threats we endure daily. Discovering through this *Course* that our experiences can be understood in a profoundly different way changes us completely.

The miracle is our changed perception about every single event. After a while it's hard to believe that we used to see every experience as though it were out to get us. Now we know that every situation is an opportunity to "teach only love." All we had to do was decide to follow the lead of others who were happier than we. In the process, we too became happier.

Today I'll rejoice that I am One with others.
My life is changed forever.

We have been called to share this message.

Whoever we are, wherever we are, it's no accident that we are here, now, carrying the message of the *Course*. Something, perhaps the urging of a friend or a passage in a book, maybe our painful perspective or a harmful relationship, led us to the teachings we now revere. And our lives have changed. We can't go back to the old solutions ever again.

This new way of seeing has smoothed the rough edges of our lives. And this transformation has been so gentle. Sometimes we wonder why it took so long to get here. So many of our past problems would never have held so much of our focus had we known what we know now. That realization makes our present awareness all the sweeter.

Sharing what we know now comes so naturally when we keep our minds on love. The more people we touch with the message, the saner and sweeter the journey for us all.

I am part of a bigger picture. Today I can do my part in saving the world by giving only love.

GLOSSARY

ATTACK. Mean-spirited words, a look of anger or disgust, or a more physical action. The ego always gives birth to attacks.

DREAM. This experience we "seem" to be having. It isn't real, but the ego insists otherwise. It is frequently, perhaps more accurately, referred to as a nightmare.

EGO. The part of our minds that knows only fear. The ego's every thought and action has grown out of fear. God did not create the ego.

FEAR. One of the two emotions available to us. The other one is love.

FORGIVENESS. Our only assignment on this journey. Our lack of forgiveness toward ourselves gives rise to our pain and sorrow, ill health, and emotional turmoil. It is the key to our knowing happiness and the thought reversal that will carry us home.

GOD. The Creator of Spirit. God is not involved with *this experience* here, but He did place the Holy Spirit in our minds as our channel back to Him.

HEALING AND HELP. The *Course* tells us that every loving thought is true; anything else is an appeal for healing and help. This is good shorthand. It tells us that any person who attacks is merely looking for healing and help.

HOLY RELATIONSHIP. One where learning partners rely on the Holy Spirit for their direction. The partners recognize when the ego wants its way and they refuse its urging.

HOLY SPIRIT. The constant voice we all carry within our minds, given to us by God when we left the Real World. Miracles happen by letting the Holy Spirit guide our thoughts and our actions.

ILLUSION. Nothing we see is real; everything is an illusion we have projected. When the ego has charge of the "projector," we see scenes that inspire fear.

JESUS. A person like ourselves who comfortably allowed the Holy Spirit to always think and act for Him. It's His words that Helen

Schucman "heard" and wrote down for the rest of us in *A Course in Miracles.*®

LOVE. The opposite of fear and best expressed through the act of forgiveness.

MIND. Our minds consist of ego, the Holy Spirit, and our Decision Maker who chooses which of the other two to listen to. Every experience is a direct reflection.

MIRACLE. A shift in perception. Miracles happen instantly and easily. Shifting our perception from one that echoes the ego's view to one that reflects the Holy Spirit's is all that's required.

NIGHTMARE. Another name for the experience we're having in this life, if the ego has its way. When we're greatly troubled, this life seems more like a nightmare than a dream.

REAL. As in Real World, God's home and ours too. What we see here and now is *not real,* but only an illusion, one that matches the perceiver's point of view.

SEPARATION. It is said that in a tiny, mad moment, the ego separated from God and this nightmare resulted. Our feeling of separation from God is mimicked repeatedly within all other relationships. We fail to see our Oneness so we cling, manipulate, and seek control. This journey is our opportunity to be holy and joined again with God.

SPECIAL RELATIONSHIP. The opposite of a holy relationship. The ego attempts to make hostages of others to avoid the fear of aloneness.

SPIRIT. God's creation and all that really exists. We are wholly Spirit; however, we have forgotten our true identity. *A Course in Miracles*® is our pathway back to the knowledge of our true selves.

THOUGHT SYSTEM. We are constantly governed by one of two thought systems. If we are feeling fear or any of its characteristics, the ego's thought system is in charge. If our hearts are forgiving, thus loving, the Holy Spirit's thought system is being reflected.

UNION. Acknowledging our Oneness with others. Joining with another to make a holy relationship.

INDEX

————————————